# LONDON

# ILLUSTRATED GEOLOGICAL WALKS

## Eric Robinson

Book Two

Photographs by Mike Gray
Maps by Colin Stuart

Published to Celebrate
the 125th Anniversary
of
The Geologists' Association

by

Scottish Academic Press
Edinburgh and London

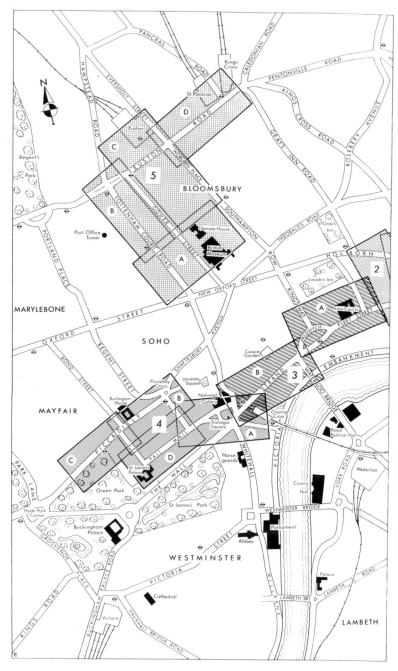

KEY MAPS TO WALKS NUMBERED 1–5

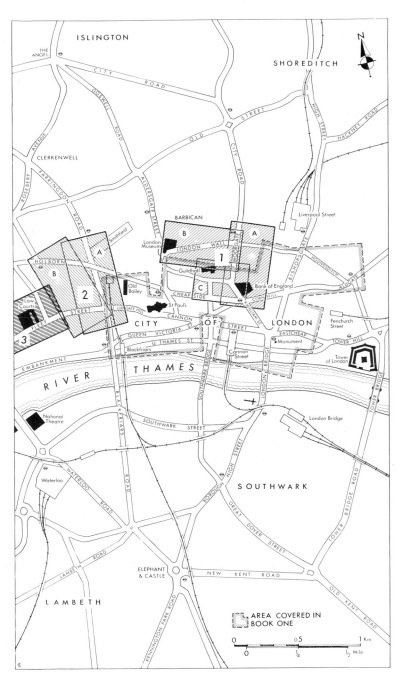

AND AREA COVERED IN BOOK ONE 1984

# LONDON
# ILLUSTRATED GEOLOGICAL WALKS

Published by
Scottish Academic Press Ltd.
33 Montgomery Street, Edinburgh EH7 5JX
for the
Geologists' Association

ISBN 0 7073 0416 4

Printed in Northern Ireland by
The Universities Press (Belfast) Ltd.

# INTRODUCTION

This second book of Geological Walks follows the pattern established in the first, transferring attention westwards from the strict limits of The City area of London to Holborn, Fleet Street and the West End. Routes have been planned and set out here in the expectation that they will be followed on foot and at a leisurely pace, so that the walker will be able to divert into byways or linger that little while longer in a manner impossible to the motorist.

It is difficult not to become aware of the constantly changing face of London streets as redevelopment sees the demolition of long familiar buildings and their replacement by new structures, often employing new materials. Sometimes there are changes of name for buildings as they change ownership. For these reasons, street numbers are mentioned in some instances, as being the more permanent record. For the more radical changes be prepared to do your own revision as events dictate. These walks were compiled in early summer 1984 and revised up to October of that year, at which time, several changes were already in train.

As much may be said about the naming of natural stones. Experience has proved that while much can be done by direct observation on the ground to determine rock types, actual proof, or the confirmation of a name from a building record, can take time. The author would be grateful for any further information from architects, builders and geologists.

Once again, acknowledgement is owed to many people: to those who have offered comment in the course of walks organised by *The Geologists' Association* and those who have shared opinions on sites, including the professionals of the stone firms with all their experience. Valuable contributions to the finished book have once again been made by Mike Gray, who worked on the photographic illustrations, and to Colin Stuart who devised the street maps. I am particularly grateful to Trevor Greensmith and Chris Green for the final editing of the text for both volumes.

*The Shaw Theatre and St Pancras Station*

*Lothbury, looking to The Stock Exchange tower; Bank of England to the right*

# THE ROYAL EXCHANGE, MOORGATE AND THE BARBICAN

This walk begins in Bartholomew Lane, between the eastern walls of the **Bank of England** (1) and the equally tall cliff of Portland Stone which is the headquarters of the **Sun Alliance Insurance Company** (2). What we see of the Bank is very limited, but it is one of the oldest surviving stretches of the late-18th, early-19th century walling of Soane's Bank, whereas most of the north and west faces which we see are the Baker restructuring of the 20th century. In Bartholomew Lane, the solid base courses and the massive fluted columns which rise from it offer us sight of old and weathered Portland Stone of almost two hundred years exposure, with rather surprising contrasts. Some of the stone for example shows some surface loss so that shell fragments stand out prominently from the blocks. Alongside there can be other blocks which still retain the mason's marks and tooling of the time of building. It is possible that these contrasts may reflect slight differences in quality in the stone, but it is much more likely that as with the weathering colour—dark or gleaming white—such contrasts are a reflection of local 'climate' and fractionally different degrees of exposure to the local agencies of weathering. What is much more directly attributable are the clumsy attempts which have been made to patch and restore wear-and-tear, including bomb-damage. This has usually involved cutting out damaged areas and filling the gap with various pastes of stone dust and cement, attempting to match both colour and texture with the original limestone. Sadly, many fills seem to have been quite badly misjudged on one count or another, especially those which included sand grains and flint chips in their make-up as these have invariably ended up darker or visibly speckled in their appearance. Biblical quotations apropos patches on old garments come to mind, but the simpler conclusion seems to be that the invisible patching of damaged masonry is a skill in but few hands.

Newer and more impressive Portland Stone is to be seen in the Sun Alliance frontage, rising from a base course of fine grained grey-blue granite which is of unknown source, but which may be Creetown Granite from Dalbeattie (in truth, a grano-diorite).

Of all the buildings in this vicinity, the one which deserves more than just a passing mention must be the **National Westminster Bank** in Lothbury (3), closing off Bartholomew Lane to the north. Designed by the architects Mewès & Davis and built in 1923, this building has two aspects to savour. First, there is the scale of the bank and the architectural details which lighten what is otherwise a massive building when viewed down the length of the Lane. The architects are otherwise best known for their work at The Ritz and The Royal Automobile Club in Pall Mall, and drew much of their inspiration from the styles of the best buildings being built in Paris. Here in Lothbury, they designed a substantial bank, well able to keep company with its neighbour across the street, and at the same time rise to a wide variety of columns, capitals and neat window surrounds, all executed in good quality Portland Stone of the best freestone quality.

The second geological virtue in this bank becomes evident when we study at close quarters the 1.5 m high base course of smooth-rubbed Cornish granite. The rock is grey from a distance but becomes browner when we look more closely at the background to the countless lath-shaped crystals of feldspar which dominate the texture. The background includes quartz and biotite and muscovite mica, all of which have a darker tone than the slender feldspars, but it is still darker fragments which tend to catch the eye and at the same time prove most interesting. At frequent intervals through the rock, there are elongate pieces of the slaty rocks which form the local crust in Cornwall ('killas') which have been caught up in the granite melt as it intruded itself into the country rock. Less frequently, there are elongate pieces of vein quartz which may have been injected within the fold cores of the killas and then later, have been incorporated themselves within the granite as a 'heathen' body. It is not certain which of the Cornish granites this rock is, but it may be from the Falmouth area.

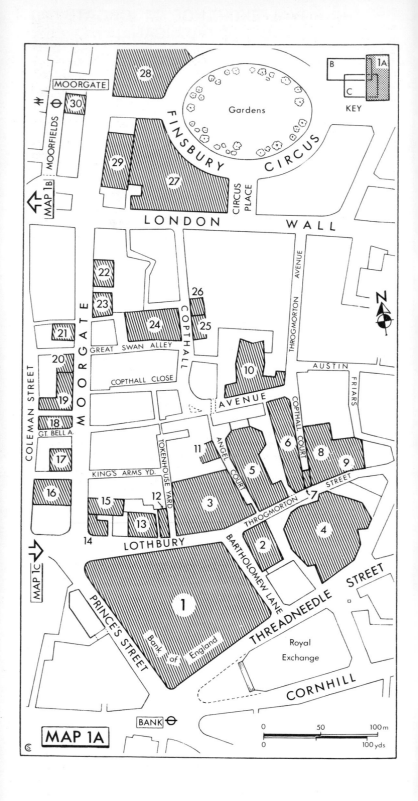

MAP 1A

From Lothbury, we move into the narrows of Throgmorton Street and to the northern margin of the **Stock Exchange** complex (**4**). Rebuilt in 1969 as an integrated series of halls and office suites by Llewellyn–Davies and Partners, this is a building which makes a signal contribution to geology in the shape of the large polished surface areas of grey Hantergantick Granite at pavement level. This finer-grained grey granite is from quarries on Bodmin Moor, an area generally lacking the large feldspar granites of southwest England, rock types which we shall see shortly in Moorgate. What strikes one particularly about Hantergantick Granite are the patch-areas of white feldspar concentrations which look like clouds from a distance. When looked at closely, you can detect a slightly indefinite outline to some of the feldspar crystals suggesting that the mineral has undergone alteration to kaolinite. We could probably agree that the granite of the Stock Exchange is not the granite of the National Westminster Bank in Lothbury.

On the north pavement of Throgmorton Street, opposite The Stock Exchange, another granite is offered in the facing to **Banque Paribas** (**5**), 30 Throgmorton Street. This is only part of the complex of banks and offices which make up Morgan House, otherwise known as Angel Court, a building characterised throughout by a combination of brown-tinted glass and smooth surfaces of polished granite. The granite is the American Dakota Mahogany Granite from an extension southwards of the Canadian Precambrian Shield into the Mid-Western states. Rich red-brown feldspars give the rock its reddish colour, offset slightly by the small blue quartz crystals and the grey tone of a second type of feldspar which together make up the majority of the rock. Seen over so many square metres of surface area, a slightly metamorphic fabric is soon evident in the panels, combined with a faint pattern of pink feldspar (aplitic) veins. Altogether, there is an attractive texture to the granite, amounting to something akin to the grain seen in polished wood, which being interpreted, allows us to appreciate that this must have been an 'older' granite, subjected to later deformation which imposed these metamorphic characteristics upon the once-simple igneous rock.

National Westminster Bank, Lothbury (**3**)

In **Warnford Court** next door (**6**), we have the opportunity to compare Imperial Mahogany with the best-known British red granite, Peterhead Granite from northern Aberdeenshire. Peterhead forms the tall door surround to this Victorian office block, rebuilt in its present form in 1884 with the rest of its fabric of now-dulled Portland Stone. The granite as seen here is even-grained, with a distinctive salmon-pink orthoclase feldspar the most prominent of its minerals. Colourless, glassy patches are space-filling quartz; greenish or black flecks are chiefly biotite mica or, less frequently, hornblende. A regular feature of the rock are the rounded dark inclusions of what was country rock (Dalradian Schists of the eastern Grampian Mountains) at the time of intrusion. These form the so-called 'heathen' of the quarrymen; the xenoliths of the more formal geologist.

Yet another red granite follows immediately after Warnford Court in the superb Baroque-style stonework of the **archway** to Copthall Court and Throgmorton Avenue beyond (**7**). The arch itself and the ground floor frontages to the restaurants and wine bars which flank the grand entrance to **Draper's Hall** (**8**), all show polished pillars and columns of rich red Swedish Imperial Granite, or possibly it may be one of the types called either 'Balmoral' or 'Bon accord'. These last names date from the late-19th century when Scandinavian granites were first coming into the trade, shipped in block to be cut, turned and polished in the stoneyards of Aberdeen. In such circumstances, names associated in any way with Royal Deeside were judged to be a useful cachet as opposed to those which would have betrayed their Swedish provenance. As it is, most Swedish or Finnish red granites are instantly recognisable for the deep red colour of their feldspars unmatched by those of Peterhead, Ross of Mull or Corennie in Britain. Furthermore, they as a rule display a degree of fracturing and deformation which has produced significant shattering within the larger feldspar crystals, which appear sliced through with small, closely spaced fractures. Most Swedish or Finnish red granites come from the root zones of the Caledonian fold mountain belt of mid- and south-central Sweden, or southern Finland—areas where deformation continued after their original intrusion. In the archway itself, the rich red granite is set off by columns of silver-flecked Larvikite, the very distinctive syenite from the shores of Oslo Fjord and virtually no other region of the World. Larvikite will always be recognisable by reason of its large iridescent feldspars which catch and reflect the light to give the characteristic sheen in any light intensity. Seen here together, these two Scandinavian rocks give an added richness to an architecture which already contrasts strongly with the simplicity of The Stock Exchange opposite, and making this part of Throgmorton Street an area of the City worthy of a conservation order from a geological point of view.

Sandwiched between the granite frontages just described, the entrance to Draper's Hall shows a combination of slightly yellowed Portland Stone and fiery red bricks, the most striking details being the large caryatids (by Sir Thomas Jackson) fashioned from the versatile Upper Jurassic limestone. To complete our range of granites within a short space, we pass on to **27 Throgmorton Street** to see pillars and panels of recently cleaned Shap Granite (**9**).

*Archway to Throgmorton Avenue from Lothbury (**7**)*

In colour, the rock is a deep reddish-brown, the whole surface being lightened by the substantial number of large orthoclase feldspar crystals which appear to float within the darker coloured matrix. This is a notable example of porphyritic texture—the Porphyry of antiquity. Like larvikite just mentioned earlier, Shap Granite is a rock unique in colour and textural character, not just in Britain but in the World, coming only from a small area of the Lake District, Wasdale Crags on Shap Fell.

Retracing our steps to Throgmorton Avenue by way of Copthall Court, we can see further Shap Granite in the door surround to the northeast entrance to Warnford Court. Opposite, is a previous headquarters building of the **National Westminster Bank** (**10**) built by Seifert in 1967 but now superseded by the newer, taller National Westminster Tower a short distance away between Old Broad Street and Bishopsgate. The stone clad parts of this building are of the usual even-grained Portland Stone of the Base- or Whit-Bed type and need no further comment, but the base course to the bank is faced with a rock referred to as 'black granite' but which, in fact, is a totally different type known as gabbro. This rock, viewed slightly obliquely in direct sunlight, quickly reveals a close spaced fabric of outlines of feldspar crystals picked out by delicate films of opaque metals. Otherwise, most of the original minerals seem to be crowded with tiny inclusions of equally black opaque ores. The provenance of this particular rock is uncertain.

On the opposite side of the private road leading to Copthall Avenue, we can now see the fullest extent of Morgan House and the Angel Court development—a tall tower springing from a substantial base-podium of offices with bulging window bays of brown glass surrounded by flush panels of Dakota Mahogany Granite (see **5** above). As a building, there are several interesting facts relating to its completion (Jones, 1979; Burton, 1982). First, the building involved some 100,000 square feet of granite cladding in slabs roughly 5'6" by 4'6" and 1'0" thick. Secondly, while conventionally these granite panels would have been fitted to the building on site by a large work force of stone fitters, here the panels were fitted in advance to prefabricated frames which were then fitted to the

Angel Court Tower

building as finished units. This system was adopted by the stone firm, Bannocks of Birmingham, to avoid some of the problems of handling a considerable tonnage of rock in the narrowly confined city centre site where working space at ground level was limited throughout the construction period.

Once again, Dakota Mahogany Granite can be seen here in extensive polished surfaces, but note also the duller 'flamed' finish to the same rock in the stairways and the stairway walls, where it is the glint of light from the cleavage surfaces of the feldspar crystals which help identify the rock with its polished version nearby.

Threading our way through the entrance approach to Morgan House, Angel Court itself survives as a quiet link between Throgmorton Avenue and Throgmorton Street. Midway between the two stands the International Commercial Bank, **Nos. 9–10 Angel Court**, an interesting contrast to the new buildings which completely surround it (**11**). A Victorian bank, this building is fronted by rounded columns of pink Peterhead Granite with column bases of near-black Rubislaw Granite, the squared bases being of the paler grey Kemnay Granite—all granites from Aberdeenshire. These colour contrasts in polished granite all serve to set off quite splendidly the pale Portland Stone of the frontage.

*Doorway to No. 7, Lothbury (**12**)*

The recently renovated entrance to the bank introduced a further rock type in the currently popular Italian Perlato Marble, a buff coloured Cretaceous limestone crowded with paler patches which turn out to be corals, calcareous algae or clumps of bryozoa.

Back in Throgmorton Street, our steps are retraced to the National Westminster Bank in Lothbury and on to the narrow fronted building, **No. 7 Lothbury** between Tokenhouse Yard and St Margaret's Close, a building which deserves several minutes attention for its geology as much as its undoubted style (**12**).

Taking style first, it is a kind of Venetian 'palazzo' which would have looked appropriate if Lothbury had been flooded and plied by gondolas rather than taxis. Fitting the standards set out by John Ruskin, it involves a number of colour contrasting rock types—red, white and purple—which help set out and emphasize the details of decoration and structure. Number 7 was built in 1866 by the architect Somers Clark (sometime the Surveyor of the Fabric of St Paul's Cathedral) for the Auction Mart Company, on a site which is incredibly confined and restricts viewing. The base courses at pavement level are pale pink New Red Sandstone, probably from quarries at Mansfield in Sherwood Forest. This is a fine grained, slightly friable stone, the surface weathering of which has caused fine sedimentary structures, including current bedding and ripple-drift crosslamination, to emerge with the passage of time. Several blocks have been replaced and some of this patching doesn't quite make a colour match. At higher floor levels, Portland Stone provides smooth ashlar walling, picked out by further use of contrasting red sandstone in pillars and in the keystone shaped blocks in the window arches. At street level, the entrance is made more imposing by the series of rounded shafts of purple veined serpentinite which, when new and fully polished, must have added a richness to the whole frontage. Unfortunately, serpentinite in external use does deteriorate over the years and really does require regular refurbishment to retain its best effect. These door pillars, however, are not the only geological 'decoration' and if we stand back and look at the tall blank wall which climbs above the roof level of the adjacent Wren church we see that its upper part is decorated with large roundels, each carrying discs of coloured marble adding a jewel-like quality to the white surfaces. Set as it is amid the Portland Stone cliffs of the nearby banks, Number 7 itself is something of a jewel in this corner of the City.

**St Margaret's Lothbury** next door (**13**), is a short-fronted, space-filling church (rebuilt 1701) clad with a skin of 'mature' Portland Stone, somewhat yellowed with age and with a neat lead spire. Most of the blocks are of freestone quality, poor in shell fragments except for one solitary block west of the door to Lothbury which is crowded with oyster shells.

The next building of geological interest stands at the foot of Moorgate, occupying the corner site, and currently the **Bank Saderat of Iran** (**14**). At pavement level, the walling is of a pecked-surfaced pink igneous rock, without the usual opportunity to appraise its mineral composition or textural characteristics in a polished surface. In spite of this it is almost certainly Peterhead Granite once more, because through the pitted surface you can make out, from place to place, small pebble-like

masses which match the usual inclusions of schist we have already noted occurring in this granite (see **6** above). The stone is quite striking in this unusual treatment, although the customary polished surfaces might have given a richer finish overall. Just such an effect is produced by the deep red panels of marble which are set back in the window and entrance bays. This could be an Italian Liassic limestone from the Apennines, but provenance is uncertain for this attractive stone.

So much for the ground floor and recent changes; when we look at the bank from the width of Lothbury or from the other side of Moorgate we can appreciate that the upper floors are very different, being of recently cleaned pale buff Bath Stone from the Middle Jurassic outcrops of the Cotswold Avon Valley.

Moving into Moorgate, **Founders Court** (**15**) is a modern building with much glass, but strong verticals which involve natural stone in the form of Blaubrun Granodiorite—an aptly named rock in which brownish tinged feldspars combine with distinctly blue quartzes. As has been mentioned in the case of some of the Swedish red granites, blueness in quartz crystals has been attributed to stress-induced fractures producing an internal reflection of light, so that blue tones indicate deformed igneous rocks. Blaubrun comes from a Caledonian deformed belt of central Sweden.

In contrast to this modern building of 1975 involving an 'exotic' igneous rock, **Basildon House** (**16**) on the opposite side of the street is a full-Baroque style office block of the 1890's employing a number of well tried granites popular at the time. Pink Peterhead Granite is the stone of the pillars about the main entrance, flanked by columns of dark blue larvikite. Peterhead again forms the massive uprights facing the building, coupled with equally massive rounded columns of dark grey foliated Rubislaw Granite, quarried within the city limits of Aberdeen. To complete the range of British granites, the steps to Moorgate are of a buff-brown, feldspar rich Cornish Granite, adding a final touch of richness to a building which demonstrates the qualities of natural stone.

Facing Basildon House across the narrow King's Arms Yard at right angles to Moorgate is a highly decorated building of Portland Stone,

*Union Bank of Nigeria Moorgate (17)*

13–15 Moorgate, currently the **Union Bank of Nigeria (17)**, designed by Aston Webb in 1890. Remembering that the same architect was responsible for the Victoria and Albert Museum (1899), the Prince Consort Road frontage to Imperial College (1909) and the east face of Buckingham Palace (1912), the bank in Moorgate seems all the more remarkable. Its surface is encrusted with carved details and groups of figures representing Trade and Industry, Justice and the Virtues, the special effect being the elaborate corner angle entrance which passes directly up into a lantern-like bow window at first and second floors. Here again we have a demonstration of the freestone qualities of Portland Stone, this time by a sculptural mason given his head.

Nor is this the end of our interest, for at pavement level this same bank offers a spectacular base course of a strikingly megacrystic Cornish granite, probably from the Land's End intrusive from the scale of the minerals. Large orthoclase feldspars can reach up to 10 cm in length, at which size they can be seen to be internally zoned by grain inclusions which suggest that they 'grew' from smaller core crystals. The whole texture is an extreme version of what we had already seen in Lothbury (see **3** above); here, it is a splendid detail in a striking building.

Beyond Great Bell Alley, 19 Moorgate, the **Zambia National Bank (18)** involves further use of dark grey Aberdeenshire granite: Kemnay Granite, a mica-rich granite from mid-Aberdeenshire, not quite so sombre in tone as Rubislaw. Panels at ground level in Moorgate are of a 'black granite' which here in fact retains the patchy texture which would suggest that it had originally been a gabbro. Its provenance is unknown.

*Detail in Portland Stone above Bank entrance (17)*

*Cornish Granite base to columns (17)*

Further up Moorgate, the **First Bank of Minneapolis (19)** has recently been refurbished at street level introducing a pale coloured marble crowded with shells, a rock which deserves our attention. The shells are of bivalve molluscs known as 'rudists'—thick-walled, cone-shaped shells which lived on the seabed in clusters after the fashion of present day oysters. As fossils, they are particular features of Upper Jurassic or Cretaceous warm seas which extended across the Mediterranean into Spain and Portugal, and, as the rock type is unknown in northern Europe, it is probably from those countries that this rock has come. Close scrutiny of the panels also reveals small corals, bryozoa and even foraminifera seen in cross section.

Since the completion of this text, this building has been completely stripped of the facing stone. It is uncertain what will replace it after the current refit. This emphasises the rapidly changing face of the City at the present time.

The **Westdeutsche Landesbanke (20)** is a building recently refaced in slabs of Baltic Brown Granite from southern Finland. The interest of this rock to the geologist is that it represents the type of granite known as 'Rapakivi', in which there are large feldspar phenocrysts which are mantled by further outgrowths of the mineral, often with a decidedly clear break in colour and structure. As an everyday term for recognition, you could say that the rock had a 'scotch egg' texture. Baltic Brown has been a popular choice in the finishing of buildings since 1980 and elsewhere in London can be seen to good advantage in Credit Suisse, Bishopsgate, or in the new E.M.I. building in Tottenham Court Road.

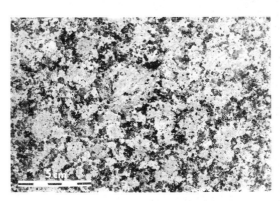

*Detail of Baltic Brown Granite (20)*

*Goldfields, 49 Moorgate (21)*

The offices of **Consolidated Goldfields**, 49 Moorgate (**21**), are of Portland Stone, but at ground floor level have large panels of deep green serpentinite criss-crossed by a dense pattern of white calcite veins. As described from its occurrence in other buildings, this rock represents intense alteration or metamorphism of original material which was igneous rock, usually of basaltic or gabbroic composition. Such alteration would take place in the crust deep within the roots of mountain chains such as the Alps, and it is from such areas as Savoy in north Italy or Thessalonika in northern Greece that most serpentinite is drawn.

At this point, it is best to cross to the east side of Moorgate to follow up geological interests, starting with the **Harris Bank** (**22**) for its panels of dark Rustenberg Gabbro, combined with an unidentified grey granite. The South African gabbro is one of several basic igneous rocks which are quarried from the well-known Bushveld Complex—a series of massive layered intrusions of gabbro and

*Serpentinite panels (21)*

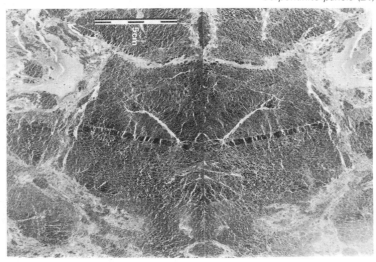

*Texas Commerce Bank, Moorgate (**23**)*

related ultrabasic rocks of Precambrian age, forming a large, saucer-shaped outcrop close to Pretoria. Further down Moorgate, the **Texas Commerce Bank** (**23**), offers a 1.5 m base course of Cornish Land's End Granite (?Lamorna) with if anything, even larger crystals of orthoclase feldspar than seen earlier in this walk in Kings Arms Yard. Being on the east side of the street this bank catches the afternoon sunshine to advantage for the study of this granite; in the case of the other bank, it is a morning study if you are to see the rock to best advantage.

At this point, we divert from Moorgate eastwards into Great Swan Alley, where we come face to face with one of the most memorable buildings of this walk. This is the headquarters of the **Institute of Chartered Accountants** (**24**), yet another building of Portland Stone, but one which is noteworthy in that it has recently been sympathetically cleaned using water spray techniques to such good effect that it positively gleams in whatever sunlight there is to brighten up the narrow street. The main reason why it is memorable, however, must be the rich sculptural decoration which

the building carries. The Institute was built in 1893 to the design of the architect, John Belcher, who was also responsible for such full-Gothic efforts as Mappin & Webb's near Mansion House. Here in Great Swan Alley, he produced a building which, with the help of others, went

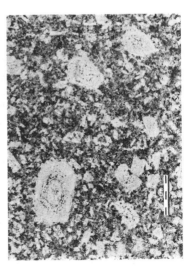

*Porphyritic granite (**23**)*

11

*Arms of Institute Chartered Accountants* (**24**)

*Portland Stone details, Great Swan Alley* (**24**)

far towards achieving the purported aims of the Art Workers Guild, to 'unify the arts of architecture, sculpture and painting . . . ' (Stamp, 1984). The decoration to the Institute both draws the eye and gives an added impression of greater height and mass. The ground and upper floors have heavy banded rustication in the smooth surfaced Portland Stone, but between the floors there is a continuous series of winsome heads, and above, just below the roofline, a continuous frieze of figures. Some are grouped together and helpfully identified as 'Education' or 'Railways'; others, however, are much more of a problem to recognise, making it a game rather like the study of the frieze to the Albert Memorial in Kensington Gardens where the famous stand shoulder to shoulder with many whose names have sunk without trace since the 1860's. The figures above Great Swan Alley (the south face of the Institute) include architects and craftsmen, among whom Sir Christopher Wren stands out for the simple reason that he holds a model of St Paul's; others are less easy to pick out. So far, all are part of the late-19th century Institute, but as we move towards Copthall Avenue we pass almost imperceptibly into the building extension of 1930, during which the frieze was also extended to include, in a more contemporary style, builders of Classical times, Greeks, Romans and Egyptians. A further building extension in 1970 received much praise, although a strong contrast with the old. It is an extension of rough-surfaced concrete uprights, with the floor levels picked out by flush panels of polished grey granite which could be either Hantergantick Granite from Bodmin Moor, or Pelastine from Falmouth. Although the change is abrupt, it must be said that the new extension hardly impairs the Victorian core to the Institute as seen in Great Swan Alley, while, seen from Copthall Avenue, it fits well into the pattern of Victorian offices and chambers looking in one direction, as much as with the Angel Court development in the other. The Institute remains, however, a monument to Portland Stone.

When we move into Copthall Avenue, we come upon more modest and traditional Victorian offices of

*Nos. 14–18 Copthall Avenue (**25**)*

some three or four storeys. These add geological details to our walk, such as further exposures of a large-feldspar Cornish Granite in the tall door surround to **Nos. 14–18 (25)**. There is nothing new here in the polished surfaces, but in the walls of the same offices we find what is clearly the same granite in rough 'axed' finish, the link between the two being the glint of light from the cleavage faces of the same large feldspar crystals. Close by, in **No. 20** Copthall Avenue **(26)**, we find again a blend of a deep red Swedish (?Imperial) Granite and columns of a dark-toned larvikite. To these features of the original chambers have been added large surface areas of the entrance foyer lined with the Italian Perlato Marble, crowded with fossils which stand out white against the pale buff body colour of this Cretaceous limestone. A final touch here are the horizontal strips of another brown-toned marble, this time Napoleon Marble from Carboniferous Limestone quarries in the Boulonnais just behind the French Channel coast. Neither of the two rocks are strictly 'marble' in the understanding of a geologist, but both are limestones which take and retain a surface polish to good effect.

Closing Copthall Avenue to the north, beyond London Wall, is **Salisbury House (27)** a substantial block of flats and offices which extends northwards into the crescent of Finsbury Circus. At street level, facing us, several shop frontages have introduced a wide range of natural and artificial materials to assert their image—intrusions which have fretted the overall fabric of the original design. Looking above this ever-changing froth the solid walls of Salisbury House stand as a demonstration of the character of Bath Stone in the City. Like the bank at the foot of Moorgate (see **14** above), the stonework here has been recently cleaned of the sooty crusts which Bath Stone tends to collect in city centre conditions, and now shows a rich orange-brown tone as it catches the sunlight. Sadly, surface pitting seems to suggest that cleaning involved sand-blasting at some stage, a process with problems for some limestones.

Circus Place leads us directly into the imposing curve of the south side of Finsbury Circus, a piece of early-19th century planning heavily overlain by 20th century aggrandisement. On the southwest side we have the continuation through of Salisbury House as a terrace of offices and

*Detail to Salisbury House, London Wall (27)*

14

*Lutyens' Britannic House, Finsbury Circus (28)*

chambers in Bath Stone. Across the long axis of the Circus comes what used to be the headquarters of British Petroleum, the original **Britannic House (28)** (now Lutyens House) before space needs obliged them to move beyond Moorfields. Architecturally, the old Britannic House is a place of pilgrimage for the admirers of the work of Edwin Lutyens (1924–27); geologically, it is another cliff of very white, mature Portland Stone with rather quirky black patches and recesses due to 'local climate'.

Leaving the Circus and turning left into Moorgate, we come to the **City of London Polytechnic (29)** housed in a building which was completed in 1903 as Electra House for a Cable and Wireless Company, thus explaining the globe-topped dome and some of the decoration to the frontage. Architecturally, Pevsner has said of the Poly that it is 'Belcher at his most intolerable . . . ', but geologically, it offers us a massive base course of axe-dressed grey Cornish Granite, made still more massive by the strong rustication which extends upwards to over 2 m above the pavement. The upper walls are of Portland Stone as might have been expected for that period. There are large feldspar granite columns flanking the grand entrance, once again from the southwest of England.

From what was common for building in the early 20th century, we find what is common for the present day when we switch across Moorgate to the new complex of shops and offices which make up the new **Moorgate Station**, completed in 1982 **(30)**. The massive pillars to Moorgate and Moorfields, as well as the walls above first floor levels, are faced in polished slabs of orange-buff Sardinian Beige Granite from the large quarries about Sassari in the northwest of the island. Of the same general age as our Cornish and Devon granites, this particular Sardinian rock has a rare colour which stems from the contained orthoclase feldspars. The fitting of the stonework in the station complex involved techniques which had been used in Angel Court previously (Burton, 1982). With the lift shafts lined with white Pentelikon Marble from Greece, the Moorgate approach is one of the grander ways to navigate towards the Barbican Centre—you

15

may get lost, but the geology is good.

The Barbican of today represents a much-delayed attempt at district planning on a grand scale, planning which commenced at the close of the Second World War. One of the undoubted bonuses from the delay, and it is as well to count these, must be the time allowed to the urban archaeologist to work out the limits and details of Roman *Londinium* and, not least, clear and display the remarkable surviving mass of the Roman City Wall, albeit borrowed from and repaired throughout Mediaeval times. Many sections are now available for study at close quarters, allowing us to note the frequency of Kentish Rag as the main component, not always in well-dressed blocks but more often as rubble stone set in a thick mortar. From time to time, there are levels where the tile-like Roman bricks are introduced to level up and bond the whole structure together against the uncontrolled tendency of rubble walling to sway out of line. Amongst the best sections for study must be those in **St Alphage's Gardens** (**31**), a short street below the walkway from Moorgate to the Barbican Art Centre. Beyond, in Wallside, the fullest height of the wall is to be seen facing **St Giles Cripplegate** across a substantial moat, particularly in the corner bastion tower (**32**), where the later, mediaeval additional courses and battlements can be seen overlying the identifiable and regular Roman masonry work.

In the second century A.D., the enclosed area of the Roman *Londinium* appears to have reached a maximum extent of some sixty acres, consolidating earlier settlements within the solid boundary of the wall. Here, in the Barbican a small separate fort straddled the present line of London Wall (the road) stretching the outline of the Roman Wall to cover the line of Aldersgate and the valley of the Ludgate stream to the west. Many details of the Roman city have emerged as central London has been rebuilt in recent years—rebuilding usually preceded by excavation wherever possible, supervised by the staff of the City of London Museum (now housed in the Barbican). Each year brings new evidence and understanding, but no discovery can have had more geological interest than that of the sunken barge

*Bastion tower to City Wall, Barbican (**32**)*

16

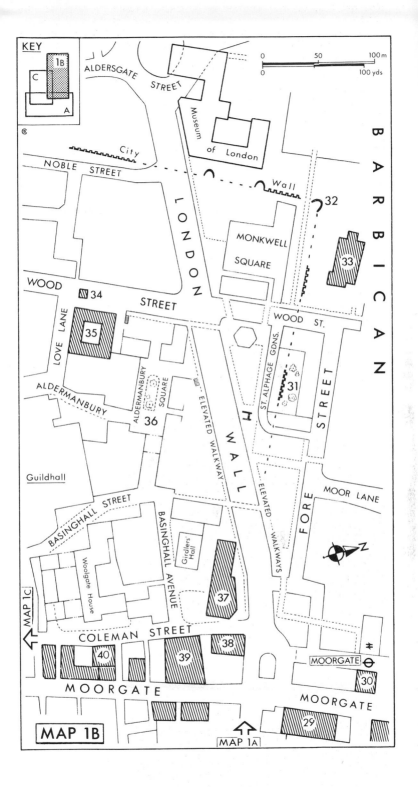

KEY

1B

C

A

©

ALDERSGATE STREET

Museum of London

City

Wall

NOBLE STREET

LONDON

MONKWELL SQUARE

32

33

BARBICAN

WOOD

34

STREET

WOOD ST.

LOVE LANE

35

ALDERMANBURY

SQUARE

ALDERMANBURY

36

ELEVATED WALKWAY

WALL

ST. ALPHAGE GDNS.

31

STREET

Guildhall

BASINGHALL STREET

Girdlers' Hall

ELEVATED WALKWAYS

FORE

MOOR LANE

N

MAP 1C

Woolgate House

BASINGHALL AVENUE

37

MOORGATE

COLEMAN STREET

38

39

40

MOORGATE

30

MOORGATE

29

MAP 1B

MAP 1A

0        50        100 m
0                  100 yds

17

*St. Giles Cripplegate, Barbican (33)*

found close to Blackfriars Bridge, complete with its cargo of Kentish Rag in transit from quarries in the Medway Valley to the inlet of the Fleet River (Marsden, 1963).

Kentish Rag figures in the fabric of **St Giles Cripplegate (33)**, a Norman foundation very much restored in Victorian times, and further rebuilt following near-total destruction during the Second World War. The buff-coloured Rag, a sandy limestone from the Lower Greensand of east Kent, seems to have been the principal building stone for all grand buildings in the South East of Britain up to the time of Wren's rebuilding of the City following the Great Fire. Then, for the first time, a wider range of limestones from Oxfordshire and the Cotswolds were brought into London, together with the Portland Stone which came from Dorset by coastal trade. In St Giles we find both traditions; the rougher surface walling displays the Ragstone, while where shape and strength matter we find the freestone-quality of Portland Stone. With its tower-topping of 17th century brick, the church forms a valuable focus as much as a contrast to the modern buildings of the Barbican which surround it. As it

stands, it is surrounded by a broad walking area paved with bricks of a different kind—dense, hard-wearing Staffordshire Brown Brindles, a variant of the well-known Staffordshire industrial brick (Staffordshire Blues) made from marls of Middle Coal Measure age from Cannock Chase in the west Midlands.

If we follow the raised walkways which are so much a feature of the Barbican, we can gain broad general views of the buildings we have been looking at more closely. For instance, from the slender footbridge which crosses London Wall there are views towards Moorgate Station, City Poly and Salisbury House. Descending on the southern side, we come directly into a close-knit pattern of streets which are a direct inheritance from the older London of Wren, the point being emphasised by the surviving tower of **St Alban's Church**, isolated upon an island in the middle of the narrow Wood Street (**34**). This was one of the eleven churches which existed within the small parish area to the north of St Paul's; all were rebuilt after 1666, but only the tower of St Alban survived damage during the Second World War.

The tower faces a relatively new

*Wood Street Police Station (35)*

**Wood Street Police Station (35)**, built in 1964 after the style of a streamlined Scotland Yard but scaled down from the archetype in Westminster. This building has but a modest base course of blue-grey granite (?Cornish Granite), before passing up into smooth finished Portland Stone which has been rusticated to give the impression of mass and solidity. There is nothing much to say about the office blocks which close up the other spaces around St Alban's. They are frame-units of the 1960's with only a token badge of natural stone at their entrances, the rest being either glass or concrete rendering.

Behind the Police Station, however, in Love Lane, there is a quiet garden which deserves a few minutes pause in our walk, as it was here that there stood the church of **St Mary Aldermanbury (36)**, rebuilt by Wren in the years between 1670–86, but destroyed by fire in 1940. Now, only the groundplan remains, with short stretches of walling standing to a height of perhaps a metre above ground level, the rest of the church having been removed stone by stone to Fulton, Missouri in the late 1960's as a

memorial to Sir Winston Churchill. Our interest in the truncated walling seen in this garden lies in the further demonstration that Wren's rebuildings after the Great Fire were usually a matter of clothing older Ragstone and rubble walling with a well-dressed exterior of Portland Stone (see St Vedast Foster in walk· 1 of Book 1).

Following the winding lane Aldermanbury northwards towards London Wall once again, we pass through an area of the City which has been opened up by new development since the 1960's, most of which is of steel framed blocks clad in Portland Stone, but all set in 'islands' set at odd angles and confined by the surviving pattern of old lanes of which Aldermanbury is one. As it continues, Aldermanbury becomes Basinghall Avenue, and at the point where it joins the 19th century Coleman Street, we find a strange set of contrasts in architecture and building materials. First, there is the compact Livery Hall of the Girdler's Company—destroyed and rebuilt after 1666; destroyed in 1940 and rebuilt in 1960. It is a classic building of its kind, with walling of russet-brown sand-faced bricks, with dressings of Portland Stone adding a brilliant white contrast. Some of the Portland Stone is of the shelly Roach type although not as cavernous as usual. It is crowded with oyster shells. Alongside and overshadowing the Hall is the long outline of **Austral House** (**37**), the offices of the National Mutual Life of Australasia. The horizontals of this building are picked out in green glass panels, but the verticals up to the second floor level are encased in veined green serpentinite. From Basinghall Avenue, Austral House is fronted by several broad flights of steps which effectively hide the lower floors, but moving round into Coleman Street, we find that the base to the building is faced with dark grey panels of what seems to be gabbro, interesting because of the frequent inclusions of black slatey rock which 'float' within the general groundmass of the igneous rock. The provenance of this rock is unknown.

The contrast with the buildings of the last stage of this walk are to be found in the Victorian commercial offices and warehouses to be seen at the head of Coleman Street facing Austral House. At the junction with

London Wall for example stands **The Armourers Hall** (**38**), of brick and stucco, capped by mouldings representing the Armourers trade and craft. Next door, **The Union Bank of India** (**39**) is a solid Portland Stone building, as is No. 74 alongside it. Both represent the idea of the time of the need to bolster the confidence of the public in the dependable character of a bank or a business through the appearance of their building. In recent years a different philosophy might be inferred, with glass walls and large picture windows making all work and transactions open to the World.

No. 67 Coleman Street is the west face of the **Westdeutsche Landesbank** of Moorgate (see **20** above) offering us once again polished surfaces of Baltic Brown Granite. Here in Coleman Street we can see more clearly the slabs of Sardinian Beige Granite which blend with the brown granite in the upper floors.

Beyond Great Swan Alley the **Allied Irish Bank** (**40**) is faced with broad panels of strongly figured travertine which is a study in itself. Like all travertines, the rock is dominated by a strong horizontal

*Allied Irish Bank,*
*Coleman Street* (**40**)

*Travertine panels at entrance to Bank (40)*

*Close-up detail, fossils in travertine (40)*

banding which is a trace of the original bedding of the deposit, some layers dense and solid limestone, other layers porous and full of cavities. In this case, the solid layers have behaved as brittle bands under stress, breaking and fracturing to produce a local breccia made the more obvious from the strong colour contrasts which exist between the layers. Another detail of this attractive rock is the presence of fossils within the matrix either as isolate specimens of bryozoa or in lens-like accumulations of gastropods. Most true travertines are non-marine spring deposits, but the presence of the fossils mentioned here would suggest that this example was not the usual Italian Tertiary travertine seen widely in London, but something more unusual. With its strong colour contrasts giving the impression of the grain of polished wood, this rather special travertine is known under the name Daino Reale, having some of the colour mottling of a roe deer. Like other travertines it comes from the Sabine Hills above Rome.

Economy and a sense of 'front' and 'back' now mean that buildings which front on to Moorgate tend to have much more modest stonework backing on to Coleman Street until we reach Kings Arms Yard with its solid Peterhead Granite offices on either side. To the west side, with the opening out of the original street to accommodate the tall blocks of **Chase Manhattan** and **Woolgate House**, and the provision of a pedestrian access route to Guildhall, we now have sight of large surface areas of dark grey Rustenberg Gabbro—the stone of the Bushveld

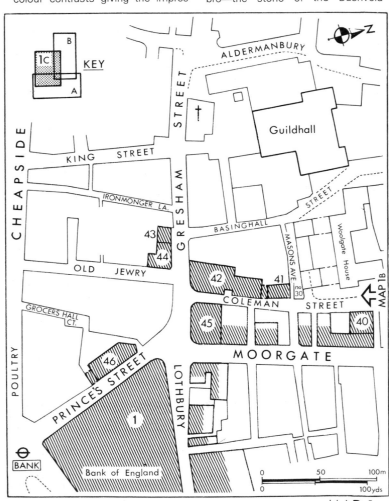

**MAP 1c**

Complex of South Africa which is so widely used in modern buildings.

Continuing on the west side of the street, we next come to Mason's Avenue, a narrow alley which now has several points of geological interest following redevelopment completed in 1981. For example, in the facing to the building of the **Selection Trust Group** (**41**), there are panels of silver-grey lustrous Otta Schist from central Norway, including narrow strips on the glass walls to the entrance hall. This rock should stay in the mind as being everyone's idea of what a metamorphic rock should look like. In this case, it was something which originally was a shale or mudstone, which was transformed by heat and pressure into this undulose surfaced schist (the lustre is chiefly the growth of mica flakes upon the surfaces which we see). The raised match-stick objects are elongate crystals of the mineral hornblende which have 'grown' within the rock as it was altered. Good surfaces of this schist are to be seen in the shop frontages along Mason's Avenue, an old City lane conserved in the development plan for the area and carried out by the Selection Trust Company. Their plan also included the refacing of the Livery Hall of the Worshipful Company of Master Masons, which appropriately is fitted out with facings of Sardinian Beige Granite. The interiors involve a delicately figured white Italian(?) Marble, also seen in the pillars and foyer walling of 30 Coleman Street.

Moving down Coleman Street, notice now the solid Peterhead Granite rising to first floor level in the offices on Kings Arms Yard, and the equally solid granite of the northwest corner of **Basildon House** seen earlier from its Moorgate side (see **16** above). These buildings which long predate the age of 'cladding', utilised thousands of tons of natural stone at a time when British quarries were in full production.

Approaching the foot of Coleman Street and its junction with Gresham Street, we come to the premises of the **Swiss Bank Corporation** (**42**) and some very large slabs of a grey foliated granite with slaty inclusions which hint that it may be Rubislaw Granite from Aberdeen. The bank was refitted in 1963, when the paler grey granite panels were introduced below the ground floor windows and into some of the pilasters. The architect David du Aberdeen records

that the granite was from Bodmin Moor, from quarries not far from those which provide the De Lank Granite which has had wide use in London. Above the 'granite level' the bank is of good quality Portland Stone with a hard crisp surface broken by only one or two decorative swags. Inside, in the entrance foyer, there is a low wall of what seems to be orange-brown Guiting Stone, a shelly Middle Jurassic limestone from Gloucestershire, characterised by a distinct bedding produced by shell debris layers alternating with shell-poor intervals.

Crossing Gresham Street, **Nos. 56–60** are shop frontages and the office of the Equity and Law Life Assurance Company (**43**), all faced in a rich red Swedish Granite. The main walling is in a rough-riven finish, but the recessed window surrounds offer the same rock in highly polished finish. Combined with the red rock at pavement level are strips of dark Rustenberg Gabbro to give a sharp colour contrast. Moving now to the corner of Old Jewry, the public house 'The Three Bucks' and what is now the **Banco Espanola de Credito** (but originally The Australian Estates Company—hence the name Estates House) (**44**), are all faced with a grey-buff coloured stone with surfaces richly covered with muscovite mica. This is the metamorphic Barge Quartzite, really a form of quartz schist, coming from the Monte Bracco area of the Italian Alpes Maritimes. These cladding slabs are relatively thin, almost tiles, the cleaved rock being remarkably durable when split from quarried blocks.

From this corner of Old Jewry we can look across to **No 1 Moorgate** (**45**), built for Northern Insurance in 1907 by Edward Mountford, the architect of the Old Bailey. There is indeed something equally massive and Piranesian about this building with its heavily arcaded ground floor, and its extremely large rounded columns which extend throughout. The work is entirely in axe-dressed grey granite, so solid that the present extensive refitting of the premises follows two extensive fires which seem to have left the exterior more or less intact (1983). The mass of the building is of Rubislaw Granite from Aberdeen, and in the course of the rebuilding, the original solid blocks have been taken out from some areas, to be sawn into 40 mm slabs to clad two additional floors to the overall structure. Even with this economy, extra material was needed for some window surrounds and space filling, for which the even-grained grey Bosahan Granite from quarries near Falmouth provided an effective match for the original Scottish stone.

Passing now down Princes Street, along the west wall of the Bank of England, the modern premises of **Manufacturers Hanover Ltd. (46)**, Nos. 7–8 Princes Street, give us another opportunity to study the Swedish Blaubrun Granite seen previously in Founders Court. In the large polished surfaces here, not only can you see the distinct brown and blue patches which give the rock its name, but moreover you can appreciate that the rock is slightly foliated (blueness in quartz may depend upon this foliation history). Inside the building the internal walls, the benching and the partitioning of the open-plan layout are all set out in coarse-grained, cavity-streaked travertine.

This modern building effectively brings us back to the Bank road intersection and our starting point, and so allows us another panoramic sweep of buildings of several different dates and styles, dominated by Portland Stone as a building material, but with a wide spectrum of other rocks making up the total mosaic.

*New and old buildings, Coleman Street*

*No. 1 Moorgate, Arab Banking Corporation of Bahrain* (**45**)

*The Prudential Assurance headquarters, Holborn,* (**21**)

# LUDGATE CIRCUS, HOLBORN VIADUCT AND FLEET STREET

Normally Ludgate Circus would hardly be considered an inspiring rendezvous for a City walk, but geologically it has some merit. Looking east, although the view is interrupted by the harsh lines of the railway viaduct, the ground rises up Ludgate Hill in a grand sweep to the plateau level on which St Paul's stands. The impeded view is to no one's satisfaction, thanks to the buildings of the Precinct at the top of the hill and to the continuing presence of the viaduct. On the credit side, the bomb-damaged lower slopes remain open space for future consideration. Given this upward slope, and the straight line of Farringdon Street at its foot, it is not difficult to visualise the natural advantages of the plateau on which Roman *Londinium* stood, further protected by the wall which ran the length of Old Bailey and the trench of the Fleet River. Before the Thames embankment was built the Thames had marshy banks and probably spilled its tidal waters in an inlet at least as far as the present Circus. Behind us, Fleet Street slopes downwards, although not quite so steeply as Ludgate Hill, from a further plateau surface of about 15 m elevation. Geographically then, we are standing on reclaimed Thames-side ground, on the line of one of the best known tributaries of the river, the Fleet. As is the case with so much of the street plan of the City, the narrow lanes and main thoroughfares are aligned with the streams, slopes, and softer ground. Those which are straight and uncompromising are for the most part Victorian, cutting across a warren of medieval beginnings.

Victorian buildings, particularly commercial warehouses and offices related to river trade, were close-packed in this ground, but with the damage sustained in the Second World War, we are now in a period of rebuilding, when new buildings and new materials are increasingly changing the character of the district. The years have also seen an increasing expansion of the newspaper industry and its ancillary trades throughout the whole area, so im-

planting still further building character into the streets and lanes. Geologically, it has bonuses in some of the striking rock types with which they advertise their presence.

The buildings of the Circus itself offer very little obvious natural stone. In this way, they are typical of the late–Victorian/Edwardian period, when brick buildings were usually encased in a stucco rendering which then could be overpainted. Details such as pediments to doors and windows, or cornices at roof level, were cast in artificial stone rather than carved from natural stone, as is the case with the swags and bearded Tritons which decorate the front of **Ludgate House** (1) in the northwest quadrant of the Circus.

To the northeast, under the shadow of the viaduct, are a group of offices which almost match Ludgate House in style, including the well-known **King Lud Tavern** (2) with some nice touches of Swedish Imperial Red Granite alongside some paintwork simulating stone, heavy brasswork and cut-glass facings. The other buildings of the Circus are best left unmentioned, except to say that there must be scope for improvement with future development. Just such effects we find when we move north along Farringdon Street on its east side and come to **Caroone House** (3), a substantial modern block completed in 1972. At pavement level, there are polished slabs of South African Rustenberg Gabbro, a rock slightly greyer in tone than other 'Black Granites' and offering a more typical gabbro texture of clusters of dark and light minerals when lit by afternoon sunlight. In the entrance to this building, the same gabbro can be seen in a smooth-axed finish in the steps and floor paving—quite a contrast to the polished finish, but definitely one and the same rock. Quite different, however, are the black horizontal bands below the first floor windows and between each floor, this being black slate, possibly Burlington Slate from the southern Lake District, the small slabs having been broken across with a semi-conchoidal fracture and set edge-wise on into

*Caroone House,*
*Farringdon Street* (**3**)

the walling.

Both from its design and stonework, Caroone House makes an important contribution to the street, contrasting with the traditional style of the **Associated Press Agency** office opposite (**4**), a building of the earlier years of this century, faced in its lower floors with a standard Cornish granite with medium sized orthoclase feldspars, the whole weathering rather grey-brown. Now **Harp House** (4/85).

Switching to the other side of the street once again, **Fleetway House** (**5**) is a newly completed building (1982), faced entirely with polished slabs of Sardinian Beige Granite from the Sassari district in the northwest part of the island. The rich orange tone of the feldspar of this rock, offset by the grey patches of quartz, gives a unique colour character to this stone, as does its equigranular texture which is not unlike that of Peterhead Granite more familiar to us. This is a building and a rock type which is best seen during afternoon daylight hours.

There are now two good reasons for crossing the road once again and climbing the steep slope of Stonecutter Street opposite. First simply to appreciate the slope of the ground and gain an understanding of the amount of down-cutting by the Fleet River into the Taplow Terrace which forms the plateau surface on either side of Farringdon Street—levels vaguely registered by the rooflines of the older buildings of the district. The second reason is to take in the buildings grouped at the top of the street, including Gotch House at the corner with St Bride Street, and the southern face of Fleet Building, the Fleet Telephone Exchange, directly to the north. **Gotch House** (**6**) is a conventional building of the late 1950's with cladding of Portland Stone which, in this case, is richer in shell debris than usual. The result is a roughness of texture as the surfaces have weathered back, leaving the shell fragments projecting. There is also a greyness of colour rather than the customary dazzling whiteness of many Portland buildings. About the entrance there are panels of rich and strongly veined green serpentinite, an elegant contrast to the limestone. **Fleet Building** (**7**) is

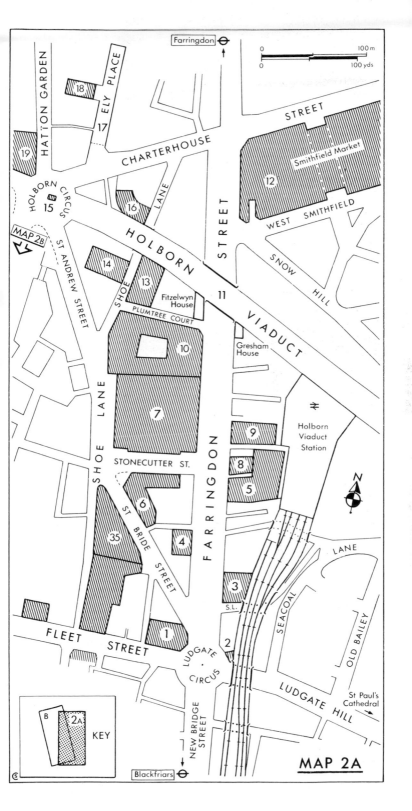

MAP 2A

*Fleetway House,
Farringdon Street* (**5**)

of roughly the same date (1958) and might easily be taken as being once again of greyish Portland Stone but closer examination of the grey slabs, especially those lining the re-entrant at the corner with St Bride's Street, will prove otherwise. The limestone is crowded with tiny crinoid ossicles, cross-sections of thin shells of *Productus* as well as the silvery shining tubules which are the spines of the same brachiopod. Clinching the Carboniferous age of this rock, there are one or two cross sections of the tabulate coral *Michelinia*, which further establish that the rock is from the Lower Carboniferous Limestone, but whether it is from British or Belgian quarries is uncertain. As in the case of the Portland Stone in Gotch House, here too there has been loss of surface from the original smooth finish, though beneath the windows the stone remains smooth and the fossils are more easy to determine. If we now follow around to the front of the Telephone Exchange in Farringdon Street, the broad flat steps are of a much more coarsely grained crinoidal limestone in which the ossicles reach up to 5 cm length—a rock akin to some which come from either Derbyshire (Wirksworth district) or Wensleydale (Richmond district). The pillars on either side of the entrance are cased in dark Ashburton or Torquay Marble, from the Middle Devonian of south Devonshire, a stone rich in fossil corals of varied shapes of colony, giving an attractive 'figure' to the stone when polished. Altogether, Fleet Building demonstrates that it does not always pay to view from a distance, and assume that all grey-white buildings are Portland Stone, thank goodness.

As we retrace our steps down Stonecutter Street, back into the valley of the Fleet, we can take in

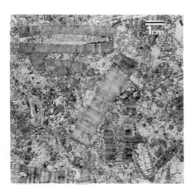

*Crinoidal limestone, Fleet Building* (**7**)

the neat character of Nos. **26–27 Farringdon Street** (**8**), an office of red brick with white stone dressings, terracotta medallions and heads, all capped by a tall Dutch gable. Built in 1886, it now stands between larger modern units of a no-nonsense simplicity compared with this typical Victorian commercial building. One of the modern buildings, Fleetway House of Barclays Bank, we have already mentioned for its Sardinian Beige Granite; to the north, **No. 30 Farringdon Street** (**9**) is of Portland Stone with small details of dark Burlington Slate about the entrance. Here, however, the impressive touch of natural stone involves panels of serpentinite so strongly net-veined as to have a leopard-skin texture.

1984 saw the completion of **Plum Tree Court** (**10**), a complete rebuilding of older premises on the west side of Farringdon Street and extending almost to Holborn Viaduct. Deeply arcaded at pavement level, with stout pillars of stone, the new building has a very Moorish quality, strengthened by the central courtyard visible beyond the entrance foyer. The uniform whiteness of surface to Plum Tree Court is achieved by the use of smooth-rubbed Empire Stone—an artificial mix using small angular chips of Portland Stone set in a cream-coloured cement. Study the pillars closely and you will see the grey blue chips of stone, and notice the absence of fossil fragments or any sign of bedding, both of which would be expected in a normal limestone. Like the pattern of a wallpaper, the even-ness of texture goes on and on.

The whiteness and the smoothness of the building is relieved between floors by elongate panels of banded travertine with a slightly greenish colour cast. A different version of the same stone has also been introduced into the interior in the form of highly polished slabs in the flooring of the foyer. This is Golden Travertine—Travertino Ascolano Oniciato Scuro—from quarries close to the Adriatic Coast of Apennine Italy (I am indebted to the Architects Dennis Lennon & Partners for this information). Like the more familiar Tivoli Travertine with its opaque cream colour, Golden Travertine is a spring deposit, but with a stronger crystalline calcite component more akin to stalagmite deposits found in caves and clearly capable of taking and retaining a polish. Its banded character is picked out by brown iron-stained layers roughly at right angles to the blade-like crystals of calcite. The highly polished wall surfaces are lined with panels of a classic Carrara Marble—a pure white limestone figured by grey diffuse veins.

Progressing up Farringdon Street, we are now almost at the foot of **Holborn Viaduct** (**11**) a geological monument which is worth savouring. As the commemorative tablet explains, the viaduct was built in 1869 as a result of the efforts of the Improvements Committee, led by Mr Thomas Henry Fry, 'to bridge the deep cut of The Fleet for traffic passing from the City to Holborn'.

*Holborn Viaduct from Farringdon Street* (**11**)

*Fitzelwyn House,
Holborn Viaduct*
**(11)**

The engineering work is impressive and is enriched by some highly decorative ironwork, now even more resplendent in plum-red paint enhanced with gilding. The arches supporting the whole structure spring from pillars of several different natural stones. Starting at pavement level, we have blocks of Cornish large-feldspar granite which are flaking upwards, seemingly as a result of salt weathering and rising damp from ground level. Above this grey base, each column has a band of black unpolished dolerite or diorite, like a black collar. The main bulk of the columns, however, is of a pink rock mottled by patches of colourless mineral which stand out against the more general pink background. The pinkness stems from orthoclase feldspar; the dark (actually colourless) patches are of quartz. The rock itself is Ross of Mull Granite. Once again, we have here an almost unique rock, distinctive compared with other granites for its reddish-pink tone and the presence of small amounts of greenish hornblende (most clearly on polished surfaces). The rock comes from the very tip of the long finger-like peninsula which juts out from Mull in Scotland towards Iona less than a mile offshore. When quarrying was

active, the trade depended entirely upon the coastal shipping fleet of the west of Scotland to shift the stone in bulk. When the working came to an end between the wars, substantial ramparts of ready squared blocks remained stacked about the worked ground (Redfern, 1979). The pillars on Farringdon Street have recently been cleaned and have lost their surface polish so as to give them a 'washed out' look. Up on the viaduct itself, the plinths to the statues to Agriculture, Commerce, Science and Fine Art retain a full polished finish and show the granite in its true colours and richness. Cleaning also seems to have taken something from the Portland Stone of the twin buildings which completed the design for the Viaduct, tall tower blocks which contain the spiral stairways from the lower to the higher levels. Both **Gresham House** (west side) and **Fitzelwyn House** (east side) are a kind of Victorian-Venetian Gothic, if such a phrase is adequate to describe their balconies supported by bearded caryatids, the fretted screens at roof level and the polished hemispheres of Peterhead Granite which bulge out from the smooth wall surfaces between the floors.

Both buildings are grouped on the

south side of the Viaduct, without any counterbalancing twins on the opposite side. This gives us an uninterrupted view northwards of the western end of **Smithfield Market (12)**, great sheds of complex ironwork but with several touches of natural stone. Most bewildering of these must be the cobbled lanes and worn pavings of the Market with a wide diversity of igneous and metamorphic rocks drawn from all parts of northern Europe in all probability. Well-worth seeing are the kerbstones and bollards at the foot of Snow Hill, and some polished panels in Market buildings, all of which are of giant-feldspar Cornish Granite, either from Carnmenellis or Penzance. At roof level, there are countless porthole-windows to the attic storey, each with a gleaming white surround of Portland Stone.

When we move westwards across the Viaduct towards Holborn we come to the **City Temple Church (13)**, a famous preaching place in nonconformist tradition, but geologically something of a demonstration of the problems of weathering in some Jurassic limestones in the London atmosphere. The church was damaged during the last war, but the frontage of heavy columns capped by a broad pediment remains pretty much in its original state, with some patching and renewal from the 1955 rebuilding. The rock is a sombre brown, except for the renewed patches which remain pale; the rock is also only sparingly fossiliferous. The colour itself is suggestive that the rock is Bath Stone, and the across-the-bedding veining (the 'watermark' of Arkell, 1947) make it almost certain that this is the case. Interestingly, there are horizontals running through the frontage and the walling above Shoe Lane to the west which are much paler in colour and which, in a weathered state, reveal quite prominent cross-bedding. These bands are also much shellier in character than the standard stone, and could be one of the 'ragstone' variants within the wide range of limestone types which we bracket together under the name Bath Stone. All these Middle Jurassic limestones were laid down in shallow water marine conditions, in some places as shell banks or limesand shoals, in others in current scoured submarine channels. It is such reconstructions of past environments which may help us under-

stand the contrasts which we see in the stone of City Temple Church.

Facing us across the deep cut of Shoe Lane is the substantial Wren church of **St Andrew's Holborn (14)** with a long simple nave and a tall square tower which may have been 'borrowed' in the details of City Temple when it was built in 1873. For once, this was a City church which was not actually damaged by the Great Fire of 1666, but for all that, it was rebuilt by Wren between 1686 and 1687 much in the style of St James's Piccadilly, or St Andrew by the Wardrobe, its older walling encased in clean-lined ashlar finished Portland Stone. Taking away the lofty modern buildings which crowd in upon it nowadays, and further removing Holborn Viaduct from the Fleet Valley, it is possible to visualise this gleaming white church as a focal point for this whole area, standing as it does upon a topographical high point in the City. Having said this, it is not now the easiest of churches to reach on weekdays, but when you can get close up, it offers the usual range of weathering aspects for Portland Stone—lightness and darkness, sharpness surviving in one place, surfaces worn back in others. If you approach from the height of the Viaduct, you will cross sandstone flagging (inevitably of Carboniferous age) which involves pieces as large in surface area as you will find anywhere in London (up to 2 m square).

Out in the centre of Holborn Circus, the statue of **Prince Albert (15)** stands on a broad oval plinth of Peterhead Granite, a point which you should verify only with considerable caution as traffic swirls about this pivot point not expecting to meet would-be geologists with their backs to the road. In fact, unless the roads are very quiet, it is probably wiser to retrace steps towards the Viaduct in order to cross close to the Portland Stone headquarters of **Chartered Consolidated (16)**. This is a building of the 1960's, built for the company, hence the decorative frieze of figures in low relief which identify its interests with things African. Geologically, we can note the even-toned buff colour of 'new' Portland Stone, several blocks which contain considerable proportions of shell debris (usually darker in colour than the matrix), and some blocks with pale spots which are small algal colonies. Moving westwards from Consoli-

*Statue of Prince Albert, Holborn Circus. Behind, British Telecom (15)*

dated brings us opposite the entrance to **Ely Place** (**17**) which is worth a visit as one of the few remaining backwaters of quiet in a very busy area. To some extent the quiet is ensured by the substantial wall which closes the Place to the north, as much as the gates and small gatehouses which check access from Holborn and the world outside. Historically this is not inappropriate, as Ely Place stands on the site of the London 'palace' of the Bishops of Ely of the 14th and 15th centuries, their chapel of that time surviving as the **Convent Church of St Etheldreda** (**18**), still linked with a present-day community. The east end of the church is slightly set back

*Ely Place from Holborn Circus (**17**)*

*Masonary, east wall, St. Etheldreda's Church (17)*

from the general line of the later 18th century town houses of the Place, and offers several points of interest to us. First, the wall is a fascinating mixture of rounded and roughly-shaped blocks of quartzite, tabular flint, Kentish Rag, possible Reigate Stone, and one or two pieces of cream coloured limestone which may be Caen Stone. Such a mixture could involve a selection from Thames Terrace Gravels as much as the recycling of quality stone from older building history between the base, left much as it might have been built by nuns with more heart than art, and the strongly contrasted smooth ashlar walling and window tracery in Bath Stone— the work of Scott when he restored the church in 1874. A further point to note, and equally evident from the pavement, is the existence of a large undercroft beneath the main chapel, its lines picked out in a lower masonry arch.

Only a short step from Ely Place and its quiet atmosphere is Hatton Garden with, at its foot, a substantial building complex which replaced the previous conglomeration of shops and offices which included Gamages. Core to the whole is No. 120 Holborn, the corner site occupied by

**British Telecom** (19). This unit, like the whole frontage, is built of substantial blocks of Stopped Travertine, used for flooring, foyer fittings, as well as pillars to the arcading to the exterior. Between the floors of this tall building there are some eight broad horizontals of polished gneiss, pinkish-brown in colour but with darker streaks running across some of the panels to emphasise its metamorphic character. Some igneous rocks which we see in buildings have clearly suffered some degree of deformation so that a weak foliation has been overprinted upon their still-recognisable granitic texture. In the case of this rock in Holborn, however, the deformation has passed to the extent that the rock displays swirling patterns of mineral alignment which are truly metamorphic in character. Having said all this, it remains uncertain where the rock originated.

On balance, the new Hatton Garden complex is a poor foil for the **Daily Mirror** building opposite (20) at the top of Fetter Lane and New Fetter Lane. Built in 1958 by the architects Owen Williams & Partners, it is aptly summed up by Ian Nairn in the phrase, 'Instead of being a weary envelope for lettable space, or good-

*The Daily Mirror building, Holborn* (**20**)

hearted fumbling after character, this is a direct, positive design'. (Nairn, 1964, p. 7.) As the printing centre for a no-holds-barred newspaper, it is a functional building with its visible pipes and conduits picked out in strong red or blue paint, all helping to emphasise its vitality. Nothing is hidden here it would seem, and geologists can share some of the architects' enthusiasm for the place on account of the diversity of natural stone which it manages to contain. Whether all the stonework blends and harmonises here is questionable.

Beginning in New Fetter Lane we have a curving wall rather like a cinema screen, which is framed in green Lake District Slate here used in rough-riven finish, these being slabs struck from larger blocks along the planes of cleavage. The rock comes from the Borrowdale Volcanic Series of Cumbria, and from the quarries at Skelwith Bridge near Ambleside which provide large quantities of this particular grade and colour tone of slate. Below this wall is a broad sill at waist level of grey Carboniferous Limestone, the same rock forming upright walling in the angle of the building to High Holborn. Oddly enough it also occurs in

the vertically scored slabs, over-painted black to make them look like slate at first glance. If you accept the Mirror's disclaimer over 'rights of way', it is worthwhile clambering on to the railed platform area in order to examine the wall surfaces of the same limestone. Here you will find cross-sections of the small coral *Zaphrentites*, the tabulate coral *Michelinia*, as well as wispy outlines of the brachiopods *Spirifer* and *Productus*, all of which effectively prove that the rock is of Lower Viséan age, although where it originated is uncertain.

Towards Holborn and the north front of the building, panels of white marble and shining gold mosaic all add to the interest of a building which is otherwise conventionally clad in grey-weathered Portland Stone. This is not the end, however, for as we approach the main entrance, we find it faced with the lustrous Otta Schist from central Norway—a high-grade metamorphic rock in which the slightly knotty surface texture is produced by the elongate crystals of the mineral hornblende which have grown within the rock. Beyond, into Fetter Lane, the pattern of Lake District Slate, Carboniferous Limestone and White Marble, is repeated, offering large surface areas for more detailed study of bedding, sedimentary structures and fossils.

Just as there seem good reasons for praising and appreciating the Daily Mirror building as 'good' for the years 1950–60, equally there could be some celebration of the **Prudential Assurance** headquarters (**21**) as being 'above standard' for 1879–1906. Admittedly, a lot depends upon whether you admire the work of Alfred Waterhouse, the architect of so many large offices and town halls in the north of England, and of course, the Natural History Museum in South Kensington. Essentially it is a building of towers and a limited number of turrets, all in fiery red brick, with mouldings and decoration in equally fiery terracotta, all underpinned by substantial ground floor use of polished red Peterhead Granite. These polished surfaces give opportunity to seek out examples of dark schist inclusions within the body of the rock, and to ponder the problem as to why there should be no obvious growth of the distinctive pink orthoclase feldspars within these 'heathen' masses when such growth is so much a feature of the inclusions within Shap Granite. The

solid pattern of the Prudential in High Holborn and its geology were exported to all provincial towns and cities in later decades as something of a trade mark and advertisement for their businesses. (Maltby, *et al.* 1983). What should now be 'exported' to all such buildings is the after-cleaning care which this Holborn granite has received. Seen in the entrance arches to the inner courtyard (security permitting) the rock surface is as if oiled and is lustrous.

A quick walk down Fetter Lane misses little of geological interest, although there is some rich, dark-coloured larvikite and Swedish Red Granite, the two separated by a collar of grey-brown Kemnay Granite, in the Edwardian decoration of the **White Horse** (**22**). When we reach the intersection of the Fetter Lanes and Rolls Buildings, we can take stock of the character of the area. In front of us to the east is the **Public Records Office** (**23**), built after the style of an enlarged Tudor College of the Henry VIIth Chapel of Westminster Abbey. The dark scaly blocks of the lower and badly weathered part of the building are Reigate Stone from the Upper Greensand of Surrey, the same rock which proved to be unsatisfactory at Westminster in

Prudential Assurance,
Peterhead Granite,
terracotta (**21**)

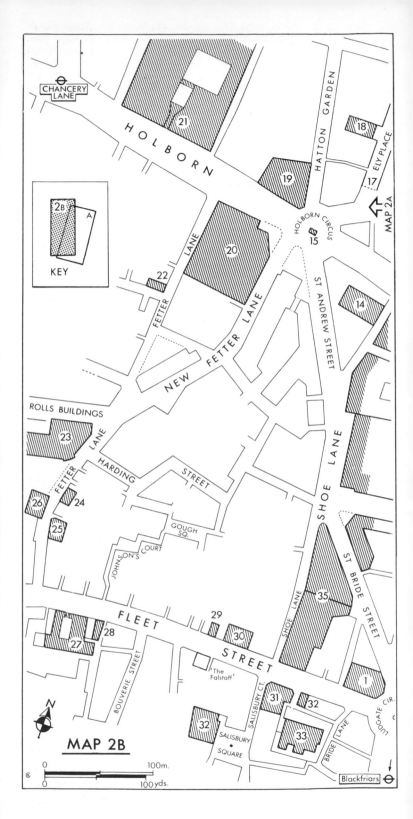

MAP 2B

CHANCERY LANE

HOLBORN

HATTON GARDEN

ELY PLACE

18

17

MAP 2A

19

HOLBORN CIRCUS

15

KEY

2B

A

20

LANE

22

FETTER

ST ANDREW STREET

14

NEW FETTER LANE

ROLLS BUILDINGS

23

LANE

SHOE LANE

FETTER

HARDING

STREET

26

24

GOUGH SQ.

25

JOHNSON'S COURT

ST BRIDE STREET

SHOE LANE

35

FLEET

29

STREET

30

27

28

BOUVERIE STREET

'The Falstaff'

SALISBURY CT.

31

32

1

LUDGATE CIR.

32

SALISBURY SQUARE

33

BRIDE LANE

N

100m.

0

100yds.

Blackfriars

the older fabric of the Abbey. Strangely, the Public Records Office was built in the 1860's at a time when there had already been several enquiries into what were the more reliable British natural stones for major buildings in the capital—enquiries initiated at the time of the rebuilding of the Houses of Parliament after the fire of 1834. For these discussions, panels of experts including the Director of the Geological Survey, professors and no less a person than William Smith himself (sometimes called 'The Father of British Geology'), were involved in the choice of Magnesian Limestone from the quarries on Bolsover Moor, near Chesterfield. This same Permian limestone had been proven to be a durable stone in several Norman castles of the north, and also in the masonry of York Minster but, unfortunately, had never previously been tested in the smoke-polluted atmosphere of a 19th-century industrialised city. When used in London, following the enquiry, the creamy-white limestone soon acquired a grimy coating of air-borne soot which in turn promoted a direct chemical attack upon the dolomite (the limestone is in fact a double carbonate of calcium and magnesium—hence the name 'Magnesian') which penetrated deeper into its surface. The long-term result of this weathering was the flaking and scaling of the stone, which has eventually caused its planned replacement by more durable limestones less prone to chemical decay. Had all this been known in the mid-19th-century, it is doubtful whether Magnesian Limestone would have been employed in this building in Fetter Lane. As it is, we have here no fewer than two stones which should have been 'rejected by the builder', standing as cautionary tales with our benefit of hindsight.

Both weaker stones contrast strongly with the crisp lines of the stonework of the upper floors and window surrounds of the same building, which are of Portland Stone. This is dark and grimy in the vertical buttresses, but gleams white in the encrusted pinnacles of the corner turrets (of a later date, and recently cleaned). As we move to the southeast corner of the Office, we come upon the second of the less successful stone choices, the yellow-buff pockmarked stone which has lost all its original sharp dressed edges and is a variety of Magnesian Limestone (Anston Stone from

*S.E. front, Public Records Office, Fetter Lane (23)*

South Yorkshire, near Worksop). To understand the geology of the Public Records Office, it is important to realise that there were two main building periods in its history, starting with the work of the architect Pennethorne between 1851 and 1866. He used Kentish Rag and Reigate Stone combined with the buff-coloured Anston Stone for the upper walling. Later, towards the end of the century, the Office was enlarged and partly restored by Sir John Taylor, who introduced the Portland Stone in place of the earlier Anston Stone, and another limestone (to be described later, when the Chancery Lane frontage is studied in the course of the Fleet Street walk) in place of the crumbling Greensand. The fusion of the two pieces of work is not regular, and if we view the south front from the locked gates to Fetter Lane, the junction can be seen rising and falling about the Tudor-style door surround. If you are fortunate enough to possess a Readers Ticket to the Record Office Library, you can enter through the security check from Chancery Lane, and study the surfaces close up, noting the decay which varies considerably from place to place in the Anston Stone details. These include full-stemmed Tudor roses and Latin inscriptions, which fade and strengthen according to exposure and protective overhangs.

Turning to the opposite side of the street, the modern blocks facing the Public Records Office could not present a stronger contrast in style of material. **No. 12–13 Fetter Lane (24)** for example is a tower of gleaming blue larvikite, pale in colour and showing all the well-known characteristics of this Norwegian Syenite—the iridescence of the large feldspar crystals and the close-knit mosaic texture of those same feldspars in the fabric of the rock. Oddly, the same rock occurs in the walling of **Citadel House** next door (**25**), but in an unusual treatment in that the rock slabs are vertically grooved from top to bottom, not just through each panel, but throughout the height of the walling. This treatment, 'ribbed and rusticated', calls for great accuracy in the machining of the rock on site, the narrow grooves being scored between equal-width sectors which, in their riven surfaces, allow us to identify the telltale feldspars and the rock as larvikite. While we can admire the skills involved, and the textural innovations which are tried these days, it is at

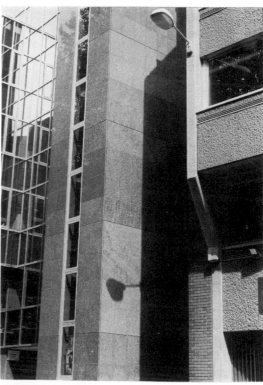

*12–13 Fetter Lane, polished Larvikite*
**(24)**

the same time difficult to avoid thinking that this is too elegant a rock to be treated in such a manner when the end effect is to produce something which could as well have been produced in artificial stone

On the opposite side of the lane **St Dunstan's House**, completed in 1979 (**26**), is faced with just such a made-up material, panels of yellow flint pebbles bonded in a mortar base, the blocks then sliced across like salami and the surfaces rubbed smooth. There is now a wide range of these composite stones on the market, most of them being crushed aggregate stone such as dolerite or basalt, Palaeozoic limestone or quartzite, all left with a rough textured surface finish. Oddest of all must be the use of burnt flint which produces a deeply cracked white 'chip' which nevertheless, as a partially fused silica rock, has high resistance to breakdown through weathering.

At this point, Fetter Lane joins Fleet Street almost at its highest point (50 m OD) from which we turn eastwards and slowly descend towards our starting point of Ludgate Circus. In doing so, we follow a City street which still retains a meandering character and is a relic of pre-Fire London and the time before an embankment held back the tidal Thames some distance to the south. At the junction, the first building to catch the eye in the midst of a mixed collection of commercial and office premises is the **Norwich Union Insurance Group** headquarters, Nos. 49–50 Fleet Street (**27**), on the south side of the street. Here we have a massive screen of columns with Corinthian capitals fronting a building of classical lines. All is carried out in grey-weathered Portland Stone, including the rugged base blocks dressed in such a way that from a distance they give the impression of being of granite, as would be the case with City banks or public buildings of any pretence.

Igneous rock occurs in the **Nigerian Commissioner's Office** (**28**), where the frontage includes grey-brown Kemnay Granite from mid-Aberdeenshire. This granite contains large flakes of muscovite mica, some of which break out into the polished surfaces with a marked silvery glint.

Most of the buildings of this section of Fleet Street will be of stones with which we are already familiar, with grey or white Portland Stone always dominant, but if you pick up the signs directing you to Dr Johnson's House, you will come upon slabs of Torquay Marble which are rather special. On either side of the narrow alley-way which leads from the northern pavement, the 'dull-but-polished' surfaces give an opportunity to study the solitary coral *Cyathophyllum* with its radiating septal structures, the colonial coral *Heliolites* with its small 'sunburst' centres set within the general tissue, and the pale but shapeless masses of calcite, which are colonies of *Stromatopora*. You can also make out areas crowded with the stem ossicles of crinoids (slender sea-lilies

*The Norwich Union Insurance, Fleet Street (**27**)*

which flourished on the flanks of the coral banks of the Devonian seas).

What follows is probably best appreciated from the pavement of the south side of Fleet Street, simply taking in the contrasts ranging from the flush-fronted Hulton House (granite in strips), the National Westminster Bank (a conventional design in Portland Stone) to a cluster of small-fronted shops and offices creating a very irregular skyline. Amongst these is No. 143 Fleet Street, Queen Mary House, otherwise identified at street level as **Trattoria Val-Ceno (29)**. The Italian facade simply cuts a swathe from the base of one of the most exaggeratedly Gothic buildings you could find in London. There are pointed windows to all floors, becoming wilder in their tracery the higher you go until, in the attic storey, you get the impression of trailing creepers with only animal life missing.

'Tastelessly and mercilessly Gothic' it may be (Pevsner, 1962, p. 323) but it is all in the versatile Portland Stone. As much is true for **The Daily Telegraph** office next door (**30**), but on a much more massive and conventional scale. At pavement level, it has the customary course of dark grey granite, but quickly passes up into a Portland Stone facade which has much in common with Victoria Coach Station. Prominent in the design are heavy fluted columns which rise from the first to the fourth floor, framed by a heavy surround which wrinkles its way to higher and higher levels. The building is at present (1985) all darkness and light, reflecting the different weathering of the limestone under wind and rain. The brightest detail must be the large gilded clock bracketed to the upper floors; but all could change with a modest cleaning operation. (completed 1985!)

From the front of the Telegraph office we get the best vantage point for viewing **Reuter's** headquarters, Nos. 82–86 Fleet Street (**31**), a building designed by Edwin Lutyens in 1935. This is a very solid-looking building which from its appearance you could believe had solid walls at least 1.5 m thick, all of very white-weathering Portland Stone. The design involves curves at the upper floor levels which can be baffling from the street below. How can a box-like tower develop concave faces to north and south? Its solid Portland faces extend unbroken from

*Restaurant Val-Ceno, Fleet Street (29)*

*Daily Telegraph,
Fleet Street* (**30**)

Fleet Street into Salisbury Court, completely shutting off all views of St Bride's Church from the main thoroughfare. Small details at the front entrance include the introduction of one of the large feldspar Cornish granites (pale coloured orthoclase crystals set in a brownish groundmass) into the steps and door surrounds.

If we now move down Salisbury Court, we come into Salisbury Square, a space dominated by Reuter's to the east, and **Fleetbank House** to the west (**32**). Of the two buildings, Reuters has lost some of its Fleet Street character, while the more modern Fleetbank House wins attention immediately for its natural stonework. The face of the newer building is crossed by strong horizontals of grey granite panels, 1–1.5 m bands separating the eight floors. In the end walls we get the best opportunity to study the rock at close quarters. What you see are polished surfaces showing lath-shaped feldspar crystals, sometimes clustered together, sometimes fanning out with greater space between them, but all suggesting fluid movement at the time of cooling of the rock. Seen from a distance in the panels of the upper floors, these

feldspar textures give the effect of white clouds against the dark grey background tone of the granite. Yet another aspect of this rock can be seen in the ground-floor panels, namely coarsely crystalline veins rich in feldspar (aplites) which cut across the other textures and clearly indicate a later episode in the history of formation. Considering all these aspects, it seem likely that this is Hantergantick Granite from Bodmin Moor—the stone employed in the rebuilding of the New Stock Exchange. It is important to note that Fleetbank House is a Civil Service establishment with security control of access but, if you peer in through the plate glass of the foyer, you will catch a glimpse of dark marble walling cut across by patterns of white calcite veins. At first glance, this rock may resemble a well-known Belgian black marble from the Ardennes, but the fossils identify it as Torquay or Ashburton Marble. This is a particularly dark coloured version of the rock which more often has a rich dark red or purple colour. Here too we have an example of stone-fitters cutting slabs from the same block of marble, opening them out edge to edge, and so producing symmetrical diamond patterns.

A final detail to Salisbury Square is the central obelisk, usually surrounded by parked cars. It is a monument to Waithman, Lord Mayor of 1823. We can see here unpolished surfaces of another Cornish granite, the large white blotches being large orthoclase feldspars, similar in many respects—chemistry, mineralogy and colour—to the granite of Fleetway House close by.

There is a quite and discreet access from Salisbury Square, through the west wing of Reuter's building, to the churchyard of **St Bride's,** bringing us face to face with a Wren church which is splendid in all respects (**33**). It has clean, simple lines, emphasised by the ashlar finish to the worn Portland Stone of its walls. It has large, light-giving windows with clear glass, augmented by large 'portholes' to the body of the church. Beyond all this, however, it has the breathtaking tower and steeple which have the form of a stone pagoda. The church is hemmed in by other buildings in such a way that it is hardly seen from Fleet Street. Reuter's we have already mentioned, but alongside is the Dalbeattie Granite and Portland Stone **Woolwich Building Society**

building (**34**), and then a whole clutter of premises right to the head of St Bride's Lane. It could be argued that St Bride's would greatly enhance the local townscape, standing as it does on a high bank to the Fleet River, if the medley of buildings to the east were levelled and it commanded Ludgate Circus. Attractive as this might seem, the close press of the 19th century buildings actually does something to support the church; to open it up could easily destroy the magic of this now-confined space with its element of surprise.

On the opposite side of Fleet Street stands **The Daily Express** building (**35**), built in 1930 and recently extended in the same style. Architecturally, the building is often praised for its clean lines and innovation in its use of materials as a truly 'modern' building. If we say that The Daily Express is 'no Daily Mirror', it should be remembered that this is a geological judgment about the building. Sadly, there is nothing original to say about glass or alloy, however skilfully combined. The interior of the foyer is lined with Italian Travertine.

*Ludgate Circus from Fleet Street*

*Rough-riven surface of Green Lake District Slate, Daily Mirror building, New Fetter Lane.*

*The Law Courts, The Strand from Temple Bar* (**24**)

# FLEET STREET, THE STRAND
## AND TRAFALGAR SQUARE

Fleet Street, the Royal processional route from Westminster to St Paul's, becomes grander at its western end about Temple Bar, both in the scale of its buildings and in its geological interest. The closing stages of the preceding walk were something of a *diminuendo* in geological terms, though if we had turned right instead of left at the foot of Fetter Lane it would have been otherwise. Westwards lie 'monuments' (buildings) galore, many of them geological gems which we can admire.

To start with, there is **Hoare's Bank (1)**, No. 37 Fleet Street, one of the oldest banks in London, predating the accepted style for Victorian banks out to impress you with their impregnability and solid worth. Instead, Hoare's Bank is in the style of the town house of a gentleman, broad-fronted, with neat and classical pediments to the windows, all carried out in somewhat sombre-toned Bath Stone. As the bank was built in 1829 to the design of Parker, sometime architect to the Bedford Estates, we can be sure that this

stone came to London by way of the Kennet and Avon Canal from some of the older quarries of the Bath area between Bath and Bradford. A brief glance at the frontage to Fleet Street is sufficient to establish that the stone involved is of a quality not always matched later in time when larger tonnages came by rail through the Great Western Railway goods yards of West London. This stone would clean well to acquire the colour of ripe corn.

Almost facing the bank on the north side of the street is the church of **St Dunstan-in-the-West (2)**, with its tower of Portland Stone a focal point for all views along Fleet Street. In fact, the tower is something of a front to the street, disguising a surprise which awaits when you take refuge from the traffic and noise through the ever-open door. Then you discover that the church is octagonal in shape, with a high-vaulted ceiling decorated with a sunburst, and with side chapels opening from each face of the octagon. Structurally, all of this was achieved

*St. Dunstan in the West, Fleet Street (2)*

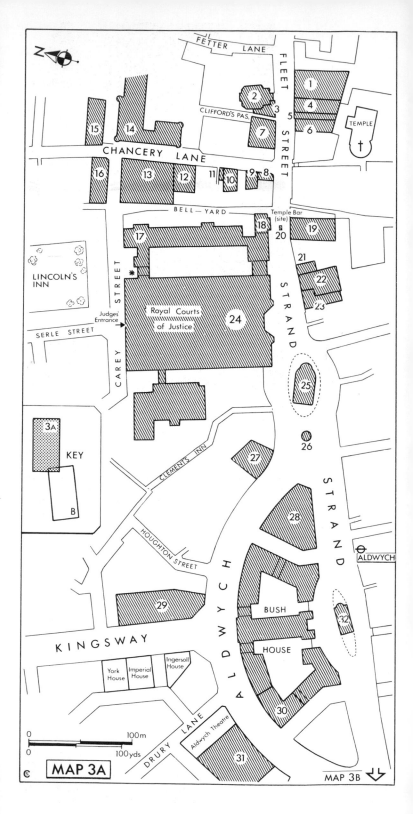

*Australian Mutual
Assurance, Fleet
Street (3)*

in brick and plaster, and for things geological we have to return to the tower. St Dunstan's was rebuilt between 1829 and 1833 by the architect John Shaw, otherwise known for early 19th-century brick built town houses. In the tower of St Dunstan's, however, he devised a striking structure which admirably demonstrates once more the qualities of first-rate Portland Stone. The tower has sheer, smooth-dressed faces decorated with a delicate ogee arch above the main entrance, with further details of a similar delicacy at belfry level. Capping it all is a crown in stone which in some ways reflects the octagon shape of the church below and creates the 'eyecatcher' of the Fleet Street skyline. Other than the stonework, there are several other details which attract the attention here, including the ancient clock flanked by the figures of Gog and Magog, springing into action on the hour. Then there is the statue of Queen Elizabeth which was originally upon Temple Bar, and the modern bust of Lord Northcliffe, whose Fleet Street patronage extended to helping with the restoration and refurbishment of this most interesting of churches.

Next door, the premises of the **Australian Mutual Provident Assurance** (**3**), have connections which deserve comment. Originally the offices of the Law Life Insurance Company, they were one of the first buildings specifically designed for a business such as insurance rather than simply adopting a town house for the purpose (Summerson, 1976). As such, these offices were designed by the same John Shaw who was responsible for St Dunstan's Church, and built in Portland Stone (1834) with very much the same discretion as seen in Hoare's Bank. The Law Life offices had as their distinctive feature slightly bowed windows, a detail copied in the more recent extension of the premises to the limit of Clifford's Inn Passage. The whole building has recently been quite sympathetically cleaned (i.e. washed and brushed down, rather than sand-blasted) so that it shines in afternoon sunlight.

From this building, we can observe three or four buildings opposite of a much bolder character, employing a wider range of building materials, all in their way reflecting ideas popular in architecture for the years 1880 to 1890. First, No. 31 Fleet Street, now the **Bradford & Bingley Building Society** (**4**), is of solid Portland Stone, liberally decorated with strapwork, attached columns and scrolls copied from Elizabethan or Jacobean buildings of some grandeur. Next, No. 29, now **Farebrothers** (**5**), combines the same Portland Stone with pilasters of very fine Peterhead Granite, the pinkness of which contrasts with the whiteness of the limestone. Then there follows, more elegant than either, No. 28, **Temple Bar House** (**6**) in which polished porphyritic Cornish Granite extends right up to first floor level then gives way to heavily rusticated Portland Stone. Seen on this scale, the granite is most impressive and invites closer study. This reveals countless examples of large feldspar crystals crowded with dark inclusions grouped in zones which serve to define stages of crystal growth. Early cores are enlarged by later additions, sometimes of a slightly different colour. Another point to observe is the orientation of the elongate crystals; parallel alignment might suggest movement of a semifluid melt, or the growth of the crystals in the solid state under a regional stress. For any of these reasons, you can profitably spend several minutes gazing at the high-vaulted entrance to No. 28 before moving on to the next geological exposures.

These are on the opposite side of the street in **Coutts Bank**, Nos. 189–190 Fleet Street (**7**), a modern intrusion into the otherwise Victorian and Edwardian sequence which we have been following up to now. Here you will find extensive surfaces of a grey-black igneous rock, highly polished and reflecting sunlight at most times of the day in such a way that the composition and mineral textures can be clearly discerned. This can be identified as gabbro by its mineral composition and texture. It is possible to make out pale clusters of minerals which from their cleavage can be recognised as plagioclase feldspars. The others are dense, black ferromagnesian and ore minerals sometimes metallic in their lustre. Nowhere is it possible to identify anything which could be recognised as quartz, so this is a silica-poor, probably basic rock. Turning to the texture, the coarse-grained dark and light minerals are clustered in an uneven fashion which is characteristic of gabbro as a rock type, so this is the broad classification which we can agree upon. Suffice to say that the stone of Coutts Bank would be 'black granite' to the Trade. In fact, this is Rustenberg Gabbro from quarries in the Bushveld Complex south of Pretoria in the Transvaal.

At the foot of Chancery Lane stands **Attenborough's** (**8**), a jewellers shop of Victorian aspect, heavy with decoration in the shape of statues, medallions, mouldings and even name-signs, all cast in a fiery

*Coutts Bank, Fleet Street* (**7**)

*Attenborough's Fleet Street (8)*

red terracotta which blends with walling of a deep pink sandstone. This same sandstone is something of a geological puzzle in that its colour is somewhat darker than that of most New Red Sandstones from the English Midlands. This may be from a more distant source such as Mauchline in Ayrshire, or the Corncockle and Locharbriggs Quarries in Dumfriesshire. To prove the point conclusively would need a specimen from Attenborough's which might reveal the millet-seed grain shapes of a wind-blown sandstone, but if such proof were to involve the demolition of this special building, let us settle for uncertainty, because on several counts, this is a building which should survive if only to sustain the geological diversity of Fleet Street.

This same aim is sustained in the buildings next door up Chancery Lane **No. 126** (**9**) is an office which has walls decorated with pseudo-Jacobean strapwork, all in a very solid, yellow-brown limestone typical of a middle Jurassic age (source unknown, and too remote from pavement level to allow close scrutiny). Next up the lane is a very colourful frontage of brick rendered in pink and white with terracotta

mouldings, including caryatids supporting the small balconies at first floor level. Diversity continues with the **Midland Bank** next door (**10**), where the ground floor involves two different grey granites, the paler of the two probably being Creetown Granite from the Dalbeattie area of the Solway Coast. The darker of the two is possibly Rubislaw Granite from Aberdeen. All of this is a modernisation of what is a Victorian office building, for if you stand back and look at it from across the Lane you will see that the upper floors involve contrasting yellow and red brick typical of that period in the City. Once again, here in a short space of Chancery Lane we have a sequence of commercial buildings which hold together quite admirably in their contrasting styles, colours and materials, a sequence to which we can add one small gratuitous fact gleaned from a trade journal. The charcoal-grey slate in the window surround of **Wilson Wright** (**11**), is Dinorwic Slate from Caernarvonshire, seen here in its rough-riven finish.

After this diversity, moving further up Chancery Lane into the heartland of the legal profession, the buildings become more formal and of mate-

*Law Fire Insurance,*
*Chancery Lane (**12**)*

rials which promise to last. All of these qualities we see in No. 114, the offices of the **Law Fire Insurance** (**12**), an italianate building with strong rustication designed by the architect Bellamy. Looking closely at the walling, note the appropriate motifs of crossed axes and fireman's helmets carved in Portland Stone. This neat and trim building is immediately followed by the more massive proportioned headquarters of the **Law Society** (**13**)—with a grey axe-dressed granite base, topped by walls and massive columns all in Portland Stone. This building was the work of Vulliamy and completed in 1831, much the same time as Wilkin's University College building in Bloomsbury. Both buildings have undergone 'cleaning' (1981–82) and both show a similar yellowing of the Portland Stone as a consequence. To clean, or not to clean?

At this point we could, until recently, have pointed to the **Public Records Office** on the other side of the Lane (**14**) as a monument to the effects of soot-laden airs upon stonework. Its front to Chancery Lane, completed in 1896, was very much a contrast in black and white, but recently (1984), this too has been cleaned. To pick up the story

where we left it in Fetter Lane (Walk 2, Ludgate Circus and Fleet Street), here there is no trace of the yellow Anston Stone or the main walling of Kentish Rag seen in the older parts of the building. Instead we have a combination of white Portland Stone in the quoins and buttresses, with a rugged bolster-dressed grey limestone in the main walling. There are fossils in this last limestone, including both corals and brachiopods, prompting a first thought that this could be Carboniferous Limestone. As usual, however, first thoughts need to be tested, and it is the fossils which seem to demonstrate that this limestone is older and from the Devonian system. In the first place, there are none of the customary Carboniferous *Productus* shells, and the corals are mainly specimens of the finger-like branching tabulate coral, *Thamnopora*, which is often prominent in the polished slabs of Devonian limestone from Torquay. The best point at which to check these features is where the northern gatepost abuts against the premises of **Wetherall, Green & Smith** (**15**) on Chancery Lane. Whatever the age of this limestone, it is unquestionably grey, making it difficult to reconcile the rock of this west front with

Public Records Office,
Chancery Lane (**14**)

Public Records Office,
detail of tower (**14**)

*Wetherall, Green & Smith, Chancery Lane* (**15**)

the phrase, 'the highly institutional red-brick of Chancery Lane'.

'The premises of Wetherall, Green & Smith' offer us extended surfaces of rough-texture Portland Stone of the Roach variety facing the newly refurbished building. Here we can see a wealth of specimens of the tall-spired gastropod *Procerithium* (the 'Portland Screw'), the large bivalve *Trigonia,* and the dense clumps of calcareous algae which make up but part of a very rich fauna of what must have been warm, limey seas. Only the last-named group of fossils (the algae), retain solid form, all the others surviving merely as casts, their solid shell having been dissolved away by acid groundwaters.

On the opposite corner of Chancery Lane with Carey Street, the **National Westminster Bank** (**16**), built as The Union Bank of London in 1865, stands as a further example of the after-effects of stone cleaning. The bank is of Portland Stone, with two solid columns of pink Peterhead Granite flanking its corner entrance though from a distance it could have been taken for a typical Middle Jurassic limestone from its warm buff colour. Moving along the Carey Street frontage, the colour

*National Westminster Bank, Chancery Lane* (**16**)

*Detail, No. 61
Carey Street (16)*

switches to a more recognisable Portland Stone whiteness, but then slips back to buff again (1984). Such is the patchiness of grime penetration into stonework that whatever the technique employed, it can be well-nigh impossible to bring a building back to a uniform 'clean' finish. This is a pity, for, as seen from the top of Bell Yard, this elegant bank could be taken to be a direct transfer of part of the Foreign Office from St James's Park to this point in Chancery Lane. As a final point to note, look at the quality of the stonework involved in the crisp details of the medallion of the old Union Bank seen above the doorway to **Bank Chambers** (No. 65 Carey Street).

If we switch now to the north pavement of Carey Street, we can view for the first time the details of the **Law Courts** (**17**), leaving the main comment on this 'monument' until we deal with its more familiar frontage to the Strand. However, we can note the changing frequency of stone to other materials in the range of buildings, as if economy and a tight budget have called the tune. As it stands, the wing closest to Bell Yard shows an equal blend of white Portland Stone with bands of strong red brickwork in a kind of blood-and-bandages alternation. The proportion of stone to brick increases as we move westwards to the arched gateway which closes off the inner courtyard (about a 50:50 ratio). Eventually, in the **Judge's Entrance** with its tall pointed gables facing on to Serle Street, all is Portland Stone, somewhat yellow. In all this frontage, two points catch the eye as points of architectural detail and stone quality. Firstly, the columns above the arch to the inner courtyard (*) begin as columns in the normal way, but then become the trunks of trees upwards, bursting into leafy foliage where normally the obligatory capital would have been. Secondly, the limestone which is elsewhere capable of a fine, smooth ashlar finish in the walling, here is freely carved into three-dimensional sculpture. What we have been looking at at close quarters now deserves to be seen in a more distant perspective by walking up Serle Street to take in the soaring roof-lines embellished with a wealth of pinnacles which help to make this a memorable building.

Retracing our steps along Carey

*Law Courts,*
*N.E. Tower,*
*Carey Street* (**17**)

*Foliage capitals,*
*Law Courts,*
*Carey Street* (**17**)

56

*Temple Bar & The Bristol and West Building Society (18)*

Street and down Bell Yard, we can now rejoin Fleet Street alongside a most impressive building with some splendid stone details. It is now the **Bristol & West Building Society (18)**, but was built by Blomfield in the years 1886–88 as the Law Courts Branch of the Bank of England with such attention to detail that it blends admirably with the adjacent Law Courts. The overall design is simple, with a broad pediment-capped front supported by two sizes of polished granite columns, flanked by tall italianate towers. All of this rises from a massively solid base of rough-dressed dark grey granite blocks. The white Portland Stone walls are in sharp contrast with the rich red granite columns mentioned already, the larger series being of porphyritic Shap Granite, the smaller being a dark toned variant of the even-grained Peterhead Granite. This last stone also enters into the fabric of the bank as shaped panels and bulging hemispheres set into the walling as a kind of stone marquetry. Seen either from east or west at this point where the road narrows into the canyon of Temple Bar, the Bristol & West with its tall perspectives effectively links the nearby fantasies of the Strand with the matter-of-fact of Fleet Street.

Standing opposite the Society building is **Williams & Glyn's Bank (19)**, designed by the architect John Gibson as Child's Bank in 1879 and forming a neat counterbalance. Earlier, Gibson had built the National Provincial Bank in Bishopsgate as a very eye-catching building of neat proportions and heavy with decorative statuary. Here, in the Strand, he devised a much more conventional building of Portland Stone with the ground floor strongly vermiculated and the upper floors rusticated.

Standing between these two buildings is **Temple Bar (20)**, the token boundary to the City which replaced the actual Temple Bar reconstructed by Wren as a triumphal arch across the processional route to St Paul's. It is doubtful whether present-day traffic would have negotiated the arches of the older Bar successfully, and there seems very little likelihood of the Wren stonework being brought back from its resting place in rural Hertfordshire for reassembly (a frequently recurring campaign by some). Meanwhile, geologists can enjoy as no one else the Victorian hotch-potch of different natural stones which stands as a substitute in the form of a traffic island. They take the form of an obelisk crowned by the Dragon of the City. The bollards at the base corners are of Shap Granite connected by panels of dark grey Rubislaw Granite, this broad base rising to an upright which appears to be Cairngall Granite. A glance at the pink feldspar crystals (rather square in outline) might remind you of those seen in the more often used Peterhead Granite of which this is a variant. Peterhead Granite itself follows on quite logically at this stage in the composite base to the obelisk. Following this flurry of granites, the main upright is of sandstone of two distinct types. The stone on the outside and corners, is pinkish and much harder than that which forms the central panel. This is unfortunate, because this panel carried the various inscriptions, and has visibly crumbled over the years. The source of both stones is uncertain, although the stronger of the two is probably from the Carboniferous, while the softer pink may well be New Red Sandstone, but this is no place to linger for prolonged debate, even when the traffic is quiter at weekends. What is more, there are good things to take in on the pavements beyond.

On the south side for example, there follows a distinguished series of banks and offices continuing on from Williams & Glyn's as far as No. 217, the Strand. Beginning with **Thanet House (21)**, we see substan-tial use of Cornish giant-feldspar granite in polished finish at both ground and first floor levels, including the massive hooded entrance. Next door, the Law Courts Branch of **Lloyds Bank (22)** has some resplendent columns of polished Peterhead Granite, demonstrating the sheer size of the granite blocks which were cut, turned and polished in Aberdeenshire at the turn of the century. Other skills of the past are seen in the giant caryatids which support the bowed balcony to the second floor. These were fashioned in terracotta as were several of the minor details of the rest of the frontage. Where the material came from is revealed when you enter the bank and look around at the walls and ceiling. All these surfaces are richly lined with patterned green, blue and white ceramic tiles, all bearing the signature 'Doulton, Lambeth'. The Lambeth Works was the source of a wide range of fired-clay wares, from monochrome heavy-duty mouldings (such as the caryatids of the bank) to the multicolour tiles and faience ware decorating the halls. Manufacture involved considerable skill in making up moulds in the first place, but equal skill was required in the controlled firing of the clays and the glazes applied to them. Originally, this building was an hotel, which helps to explain the imposing entrance hall with its solid pillars of richly coloured antique marble. In Edwardian times, such entrances were a prerequisite for restaurants and Grand Hotels.

*The Law Courts & Temple Bar, The Strand*

*Screen to the Law Courts, The Strand* (**24**)

Next door, the Strand Branch of the **National Westminster Bank** (**23**), sustains impressiveness through its massive facings of a deep red Peterhead Granite, to which are added turned columns of dark grey Rubislaw Granite at ground floor level.

At this point, we are well placed to take in the towers, turrets and the steep-pitched roof lines of the **Law Courts** opposite (**24**), built after one of the most discussed architectural competitions of Victorian times to a modified design of G. E. Street. What might have been here, we can now appreciate from the several unsuccessful designs included in the book, *London As It Might Have Been* (Barker & Hyde, 1982). What is here can be staggering, even to those who don't particularly like the eventual building, simply for the way in which it catches the eye in any view along Fleet Street or the Strand. Framed by other buildings of somewhat later date, it always seems to succeed in its perspectives as if all the possible angles had been taken into account in the first instance.

Certainly, it is a building which is recognised with approval by European visitors in summer months as they trudge towards St Paul's. After endless blocks of sheer surfaced Portland Stone, its Gothic difference as much as anything must seem encouragement to them to press on. Although Street himself was a supporter of the Arts and Crafts Guild, the Law Courts as we see them carry very little in the way of exuberant decoration. Although there are many niches, there are hardly any statues occupying them, and the mason-work is largely confined to the leafy foliage on capitals and arch mouldings. The details which most appeal, at least to the geologist, must be the open arcading which rises above the main entrance to the Strand, and the detail of the easternmost turret which overlooks Bell Yard. Follow the line of this down with your eye and you will find that it naturally connects with a slender shaft to give the silhouette of a stalked tulip. Needless to say, all this stonework is carried out in Portland Stone, but as in other Victorian projects, other stones were involved if only for their contrasting colour contribution to the overall design. In the case of the Law Courts, the prominent contrast is provided by shafts of New Red Sandstone as pillars in the long screen which faces on to the Strand, and in a number of turned columns attached to the main building. New Red Sandstone is relatively easy to work, lengths cut with the natural bedding being capable of fashioning into columns by being turned on stone lathes. Problems can arise, however, when such columns, with their natural 'grain' running the length of the shaft, are exposed to frost, rain-drip and sun drying. In these circumstances, face bedding, the alignment of natural bedding in stone with verticals in a building, can produce some catastrophic breaking away of layers of dressed stone—effects which can be seen. Such decay has been the cause of certain 'dental repairs' clearly visible in some columns, and of the resort to a red stucco rendering in other situations. Apart from the red sandstone, the main entrance to The Law Courts is flanked by columns of polished granite, the pink being Peterhead Granite (the rounded columns) and the grey being one of the large feldspar Cornish Granites (octagonal columns). Inside, within the high corridors and lofty main hall, there are several touches of different imported marbles.

It is said that the architect Street fretted himself to an early grave over the cuts and economies he was pressed to make in completing his work, a situation directly comparable with the history of St Pancras Station in a later decade. Some of the problems with the Law Courts came at an early stage in construction, and were to do with the subterranean drainage of the site. The terrace gravels on which The Strand is built form a thin skin over unpredictable London Clay—a major problem for foundation stability in the case of a large, weighty structure. At the time, however, there came a small geological bonus in the shape of the discovery of a fossil fauna, including new species, which was described in the *Proceedings* of a newly formed Geologists' Association (1874).

Leaving the Law Courts, we come to the limit of the Aldwych with the church of **St Clement Danes** (**25**) standing on an island site which divides the traffic entering and leaving the Strand. It isn't always easy to see a Wren church freed from the crush of other buildings, so allowing us views from all angles, but this is the exception. Of the exterior and geology of the church, there is very little to add to comments already passed upon other Portland Stone buildings of similar age, but having said that, we do well to take in the unique lantern-style culmination to the west tower, and remind ourselves that no two Wren churches seem to repeat the same design. While not strictly geology, it is also worthwhile looking inside St Clement in order to appreciate the skilful way in which the roof and the aisles are carried through into a rounded apse-end without a break. The interrelating surfaces are further elaborated by the plasterwork of the roof, carefully restored following war-time damage.

While there are no geological puzzles in St Clement Danes, there are a great deal in the **Gladstone Statue** which stands to the west (**26**), fending off the too-swiftly-flowing traffic from the Aldwych. Granted that he stands upon a plinth of undoubted Portland Stone, the puzzle concerns the lowermost steps of the base, which are of a brittle limestone, as white as any Portland, but different in two respects. Firstly, there are here and there darker patches and shapes in outline which are trace-fossils,—burrows created by mud-eating animals whilst the sediment was still soft. Secondly, looking at the rise of the steps, you can make out undulose surfaces running through the rock parallel to the bedding. These are solution effects produced when the limestone was still soft mud. The limestone seems certainly of Jurassic age from the small hexacorals which it sparringly contains, but whether it is a less-often seen variety from the Portland quarries would require an expert to affirm.

From the Gladstone statue, we can take in a panoramic survey of the surrounding buildings, taking in an age span of some seventy years of changing styles and materials. The D-shaped plan of the Aldwych was the outcome of yet another architectural competition at the turn of the century, aimed at improving the traffic flow to and from the City. At the same time, it aimed to clear the clutter of older and derelict buildings which had grown up south of Lincoln's Inn Fields and Drury Lane. A plan was decided upon in 1900–1901 which then initiated the building of the completely new offices and hotels to the uniformly grand scale (which we might well call 'Imperial') which give the area its unity in scale and building material.

*Australia House, The Strand (28)*

**Clement House** immediately to the north of us (**27**) belongs to the earliest period, built in 1911 for the General Insurance Company. The architect was John Burnet, who elsewhere was responsible for the north wing (the Edward VIIth Galleries) of the British Museum, Bloomsbury. In his Aldwych building, he produced a solid looking building of Portland Stone, fronted by two massive rounded pillars of grey granite, probably from Aberdeenshire, but difficult to prove on account of the fine-axed finish to the stone. The entrance is capped by a broken pediment, the separate wings of which support reclining figures which might have been borrowed from the Medici Chapel in Florence. Here, they simply balance uncomfortably over the Aldwych. If the granite of the pillars is uncertain, no such problem is posed by the dark stone forming the steps to the entrance. These are slabs of 'Petit Granit', a dark Carboniferous Limestone, probably from Belgium, named as if it were an igneous rock on account of the resemblance between the fractured surfaces of crinoid ossicles, and feldspar crystals.

Continuing our sweep of the area, directly facing us is **Australia House** (**28**), built at about the same time, 1912–1918, as a wedge-shaped building of Portland Stone, decorated with heavy statuary. It is the dull grey base-course to the building, however, which must draw our attention, for it is Bowral 'Trachyte' from New South Wales. Seen at close quarters, and in the unpolished surface finish, the main feature we notice is a rough surface pitted by small brown spots which were originally the mineral hornblende. Bowral 'Trachyte' by name would be technically a lava, but recently the rock has been reappraised as a microsyenite—an intrusive igneous rock found in smaller scale intrusive bodies. In British terms this would make it comparable with say the Threlkeld Microgranite of the Lake District, or any of the small intrusives of Snowdonia such as the 'granite' of Penmaenmawr. When polished, the Bowral stone contributes the grey-green elements to a rich display of marbles in the flooring of the entrance to Australia House, extending through into the Reading Room. This is open to the public, but the entrance itself, with the finest display, is something of a security area, not open to casual visits. There are two kinds of marble involved in the design to this imposing entrance hall, and both of them are Australian. First, there is a grey-brown limestone with paler, cloud-like patches and pale red veining. It does contain fossils—tabulate corals and bryozoa which are sufficient to guarantee its Devonian age. This is Buchan Fawn Marble, quarried from the outcrops of the Buchan Series (Devonian) of Victoria state. The second marble is basically creamy-white, with thin wisps of purple and red running through it. This is Caleula Marble from New South Wales, and, once again, is of Upper Palaeozoic age. Compared with the Buchan Marble, this second stone is a thoroughly transformed limestone, which has been both deformed and recrystallised as would be the case in a true marble. Marble used in this fashion in patterned floors and in substantial pillars to the entrance to buildings, was very much a feature of buildings of the first thirty years of this century—any Lyon's Corner House for example. A later generation sees greater open space in foyers and much simpler designs overall. For these reasons, it is worthwhile peering discreetly into the doorways of Australia House at less busy times of day.

Moving northwards, we come to the foot of **Kingsway**, a broad thoroughfare which was a later addition to the Aldwych scheme. It continues the pattern of substantial buildings in Portland Stone (**Ingersoll House, Imperial House,** and **York House**) all completed about the same time (1914–19) and mostly the work of the architects Trehearne, Norman and Partners. Adastral House on the east corner site (**29**), and now called **St Catherine's House**, is a little different in that it has surfaces of dark grey Kemnay Granite in panels which face the corner on to the Aldwych.

Behind us, **Bush House** came late on to the scene (1930), but completes the plan with its impressive recessed arch standing precisely on the axis of Kingsway. All parts of Bush House, including the sculptural work, are of Portland Stone, cream-coloured and of good quality. This state of affairs continues around the curve of The Aldwych into the slightly older **India House (30)**. Here, the normal flush walling is broken by small details of ornament which add touches appropriate to the place. The window surrounds to the second floor, for example, are framed by garlands of flowers which seem to be more Indian than the customary English swags of roses. The same is certainly true of the fretworked balcony screens (all in stone) of the third floor. Most Indian of all are the limestone lions which squat on the top of slender shafts of granite, in turn supported at pavement level on the backs of elephants. The grey granite is of unknown source, but it seems probable that the 'black granite' which forms a frame to the doorway could be from India—the source of several different varieties of this type of igneous rock. There is no trace of the mineral quartz in this rock and originally it was probably ultrabasic, possibly from the Precambrian Shield of southern India.

From India House, you can take in the character and setting of the **Waldorf Hotel** opposite (**31**), a grand hotel of Edwardian times (1906) with an appropriately grand architectural style. Heavy with Portland Stone, it rises from an Aberdeen Granite base to a rich decorative frieze and upper floor capped by a row of substantial

*St Mary-le-Strand, The Aldwych, October 1984* (**32**)

*Inveresk House, The Aldwych (33)*

urns, all in white limestone. To either side of the Waldorf you might notice that the **Aldwych** and the **Strand** Theatres are mirror images of one another, achieving their substance through Portland Stone and terracotta (note the decorative friezes moulded in that material).

Crossing the Strand, with a sideways glance at the neat outline of **St Mary-le-Strand (32)**, another Portland Stone church recently cleaned and partly restored, we can take up a position at the approach to Waterloo Bridge and survey the buildings which surround this very busy traffic intersection. Directly to the north of us stands Lloyds Bank which was a building designed by Mewes and Davis while they were still working on the Ritz at Green Park (1907). As **Inveresk House (33)**, it was built for the offices of 'The Morning Post' before all newspapers were siphoned off or banished to Fleet Street, where their architecture became strictly functional, or brash and proud of it. There is much about Inveresk House which deserves attention. The strong string course which runs across the walls and the line of the heavy mouldings to the windows draws the eye towards the curve of the Aldwych. Geologically, the lower half of the building, including many of the decorative details, are all fashioned in axe-dressed granite which often sparkles in the sunlight as its mica flakes catch the light. The rock is Iddefjord Granite from the eastern shores of the Oslo Fjord, on the Norwegian-Swedish border. This is a pale silver-grey granite, somewhat lighter in tone than the average Cornish Granite or the granodiorites from the Southern Uplands of Scotland. It seems to have been the favourite choice of these two architects, featuring in most of their work in London at the turn of the century (including the Ritz, and the R.A.C. Club).

On the opposite side of Wellington Street, facing the bank, **The Wellington** public house (**34**) is faced at ground floor level with yet another Scandinavian granite, this time a brick-red, coarsely crystalline type called variously Balmoral, Swedish Red, or Red Bon Accord in the trade literature. The depth of colour is decidedly non-British and would point to Sweden or Finland as the probable source. The rock has two kinds of feldspar crystals one of which is deep red and opaque, so giving the rock overall its strong body colour. The darker quartz can be picked out easily. The surfaces of The Wellington facing south are particularly rewarding to study in good sunlight.

The other corners of this busy crossing are pretty undistinguished by comparison, both geologically and architecturally. This is in part a reflection of the fact that many of them are 'space-fillers' of the 1950's and 1960's. One of these, **Wellington House** (**35**), is Portland Stone-faced, with small touches of larvikite and 'black granite' at pavement level in Horne's to relieve the pale cream uniformity of the limestone. There is more variety in the late-Victorian offices of 1891, packing the corner site against the solid mass of Somerset House. The main fabric is of New Red Sandstone combined with terracotta in the mouldings and attached decoration. The office of the **Britannia Building Society** (**36**) has pilasters and panels of pink Peterhead Granite which contrast with others of dark grey Rubislaw Granite—a mixture very popular with Victorian architects. Having mentioned **Somerset House** (**37**), this is probably the appropriate point at which to pass comment upon this well-known landmark. While architecturally and historically of considerable interest (it originally housed many of the early scientific societies as well as their collections of specimens as an early 19th century museum), it has to be said that in all its parts it is Portland Stone which is 'good quality' but not exceptional. The best of Somerset House is the west wing facing on to the Strand added in 1856 by Pennethorne to the core of the older buildings designed by Chambers (1776). Cleaned, and with the sculptural groups of the pediment picked out in fresh colour, this west wing is quite impressive, if only because it is set back from the road sufficiently to allow it to be seen in proper perspective.

Returning to the west side of the intersection, the geology of the western continuation of The Strand is rather patchy, as is the architecture, with a lot of indifferent buildings coupled with a dearth of natural building stone. For this reason, progress can be relatively swift towards Trafalgar Square, with only short stops on the south pavement. Our first stop is at the office of the **Western Australia Govern-**

**ment**, No. 113 The Strand at the top of Savoy Street (**38**). What we see here could be imported Australian stone in the broad window-capping strip and in the doorway. This is a grey, unfossiliferous limestone which could be Buchan Marble from Victoria. The stone of the doorway is a deep green volcanic rock, with the fine grained texture of a lava, only relieved by occasional calcite-filled vesicles which are responsible for the white flecks on the surface. It seems that this could be a fine-grained version of the Bowral 'Trachyte' once more, a stone seen already in Australia House. Certainly, there is no obvious British rock which is comparable either in colour or in texture to this particular stone.

At this point, **Savoy Street** pitches steeply down to the Embankment and Thames-side, retaining its 19th century cobbles as a further challenge to identify a possible source for what are predominantly metamorphic rock types. A full history of London street cobbles is yet to be written, but basically it would be the story of importation of already squared and dressed 'setts' by sea from a number of well-established sources, all bound up with balancing up incoming with outgoing cargo shipments from the Port of London. The bulk of the trade was with ports in Scandinavia and the Baltic, so that most of the cobbles which we now see polished clearly show banded metamorphic textures of gneisses and schists from the Precambrian or Caledonide Shields of northern Europe. Granites from the same area had a slightly higher valuation, but do figure in the dressed and shaped kerbstones of the streets. Here we find alternative sources including the Channel Islands and Brittany coming into our reckoning, along with home-grown options from Cornwall, or the Midlands. These last rocks include West Midlands dolerites ('bluestones') and the dull red stone from Mountsorrel, stone which largely came to London by way of the Grand Union Canal. The study of cobbles and kerbstones is best reserved for the quieter back streets and mews of the city, but Savoy Hill in front of us is as good as anywhere. Following it downhill, you will soon come to the **Savoy Chapel** of 1510 (**39**) with its walling of roughly dressed Kentish Rag thickly caked with a sooty weathered crust. Now the chapel of The Royal Victorian Order (since

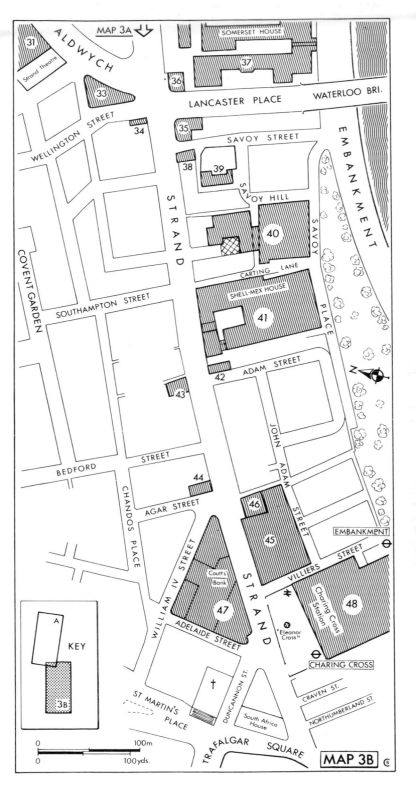

1956), its churchyard with a modest collection of gravestones grouped about the railings is another quiet refuge in this busy quarter of London.

Back in the Strand, we next come to the backwater which is the approach to the **Savoy Hotel** (**40**). Just a short distance into this cul-de-sac we meet the first natural stone, Green Lake District Slate, forming the pavement fronting the shops and the foyer to the Savoy Theatre. This northern face to the hotel (and the Strand frontage as far as *The Coal Hole*) was designed by Colcutt in 1904, and built with the most successful of the Doulton building materials, known as Carraraware. This is unique amongst ceramic tiling for its rich ivory finish, much more marble-like than high-lustre glazes of available alternatives. If we look above the chromium front to the entrance canopy to the Savoy Hotel, we can see that the same Carraraware continues up in columns to arches at roof level, the spandrels crowded with reclining figures, all cast in the same material.

At ground level, the cleaned front to the hotel shows panels of green, veined serpentinite, with strips of lustrous larvikite at pavement level. The rounded columns are in Portland Stone, but the dark green, squared collars are of basic igneous rock, which is thought to be Swedish Herrestad Diorite, a much-altered rock with a history of alteration similar to that for 'black granite' generally.

We next come to the long frontage of **Shell–Mex House** (**41**), a building which is really two combined into one. The part which we probably know best is the white tower with its clock face with skeleton numbers. This pure 1930's design caps a sheer white cliff of Portland Stone which rises from Embankment Gardens and dominates the panorama of the Embankment as seen from South Bank. Here on the Strand there is no such clear identification, for what we see fronting the street is the much older range of buildings which were originally the Cecil Hotel of 1886, and which now form a screen and gateway to the courtyard of the white tower. The Strand frontage takes in a whole sequence of shop fronts unified by a regular series of pillars of pink Peterhead Granite, coupled with bases of silver-grey larvikite. The covered entrance to the 1931 building is flanked by larger rounded pillars of Peterhead Granite, several showing large, dark-coloured inclusions of Scottish Highland schist ('heathen').

Beyond Shell–Mex House the office of **The Abbey National Building Society** (**42**), on the corner of Adam Street, is faced in silver-grey stone which is Sardinian Grey Granite added to older, darker panels of Dalbeattie Granodiorite. A comparison of the mineral texture of the two rocks would demonstrate the very close similarity between them, the principal difference remaining the warm tone of the feldspar in

*Barclays Bank, The Strand (centre right)* (**43**)

*Zimbabwe House, The Strand* (**44**)

the former and the flat grey tone of the same mineral in the other. From this point, on the northern pavement opposite, The Strand suddenly takes on a new interest. The upturn begins with **Barclays Bank** (**43**), No. 419 The Strand. This is a building of two distinct parts, the upper and greater of which is all in Portland Stone, complete with decorated bull's eye windows. With its steep pitched Mansard roof and thick green slating, the bank could have been transported bodily from a Paris boulevard. At ground floor level we can see details in a strongly patterned marble of amber-yellow tone 'figured' with concentric rings of ochreous brown pigment. This is one of the 'Onyx Marbles' of the type which often seem to come from Algeria or other parts of North Africa. Like travertines, they have a history of formation associated with cave or spring deposits on a large scale. As materials, they are often quite 'flinty' compared with normal limestones.

A short distance to the west of the bank, our next stop is **Zimbabwe House** (**44**), No. 429 the Strand, a building best viewed from the south side of the street and then later at closer quarters. From ground level to above the second floor, the building is solidly of a grey Cornish Granite rubbed smooth to a height of about 2 m above the pavement, but then treated with a fine-axed finish at higher levels. Study of the polished surfaces will reveal feldspars and a yellowish-tone to the groundmass reminiscent of other non-porphyritic

Cornish granites seen earlier. As a building, Zimbabwe House has often been discussed for its architectural merit, usually under one of its previous names of either **Rhodesia House**, or as the original headquarters of the **British Medical Association** (1907), designed by a young Charles Holden. Undoubtedly most of the comment on this building, whatever its name at the time, has attached to the attenuated nude figures grouped at third floor level. These represent The Ages of Man, and were among the earliest works of Epstein commissioned in London, and from the very start provoked a whole series of protests. Remarkably, they survived intact until 1938, when there was concern over a degree of flaking and the threat that fragments might fall to the Strand pavement below. The threat was resolved by systematically decapitating each and every figure with a Cromwellian thoroughness, leaving other anatomical parts unscathed. Geologically, it would seem that they were fashioned in the same granite as the walling below, but it has been recorded that they were of 'sandstone' (Byron, 1981). In terms of architectural history, it is slightly ironic that the same architect, Charles Holden, was later to give us the mausolean mass of Senate House and the London Transport headquarters in St James's.

Returning to the south side of the Strand, there is a geological bonus to be found in the building complex which is **Villiers House** (**45**), extending all the way to the front of Charing Cross Station. The geological points to note come in the series of shop fronts which back the pavement, starting with the end wall facing onto the steps to George Court. This is a rather washed-out looking white-surfaced marble with winding black veins which, seen from a distance, could be taken for rather drunken aerosol graffiti. Close quarters examination shows that the veins are of dark coloured calcite, slightly tougher than that of the rock itself so that the veins stand slightly raised above the general surface. Running diagonally to the sinuous curves of the veins, a faint fabric is picked out in paler streaks against the grey colour of the rock. We need to go along to the main entrance of Villiers House to see the same rock in a polished surface finish, when the fabric just described becomes much clearer. This demonstrates quite clearly that the rock we are looking at is a true marble—originally a limestone, later deformed and re-crystallised, veined, then further deformed to reach the condition seen here. The rock is Bardiglio Fiorita Marble from the Jurassic rocks of the Lucca area, some distance to the south of the well-known Carrara quarries.

Villiers House includes the office of the **State of South Australia** (**46**), in the entrance of which is a rock of deep red colour. At first glance it has much of the character of a dense, fine-grained lava, or possibly a volcanic ash comparable with our Lake District Borrowdale Volcanic Series. When you examine the surfaces with a hand-lens, however, what you see is no feldspar laths or wisps of broken lava, but rather paler specks which turn out to be tiny crinoid ossicles. This makes it clear that this is anything but a volcanic rock and in fact is a fine grained detrital limestone of unknown provenance.

Across the Strand from Villiers House is the refurbished shopping area of **West Strand** (**47**), a unit of townscape originally designed by John Nash as part of his overall plan for Central London and eventually completed in 1830 by Smirke. The development occupied a triangular site between the Strand, Adelaide Street and King William IVth Street, with a distinctive round tower or 'pepper-pot' at each of the corners. The uniform frontages were stucco-rendered after the fashion of the time. Recently, as the general state of the stucco facing began to crumble (as a finish, it does require refurbishing at intervals of time to maintain not only appearances but also its protection to the underlying fabric of a building), pressures built up for the redevelopment of the entire site, including plans to replace the older structure with a modern building, and another to make way for a four-lane motorway to relieve local traffic congestion. Following an enquiry in 1971, the decision was made to rebuild the interior space

*West Strand* (**47**)

without disturbing the long-familiar Nash exterior—a course often followed nowadays when dealing with listed buildings. The plan was eventually modified to allow **Coutts Bank** to totally restructure its central property within the triangle, breaking both line and continuity of material. The present brown glass-fronted central section to West Strand was the outcome of the architectural competition which followed the enquiry, and was a solution which won widespread approval for its ingenuity. From a geological point of view, we can note that the extensive floor and wall areas are surfaced with the attractive cream coloured Italian Botticino Marble, including the escalator ramps, and the curved surfaces of foyer desks and counters. Cretaceous fossils, sedimentary structures and limestone textures are all visible here.

**Charing Cross Station (48)** faces the Strand in the shape of its even-fronted brick-built hotel, set back above its open courtyard in which the replacement Eleanor Cross is a focal point. The hotel was designed by E. M. Barry in 1869 in a style which befitted a railway offering journeys to Continental destinations, but as it was built in yellow stock brick with copious details fashioned in some form of artificial stone, the hotel is less interesting to us than the cobbled forecourt. It is usually safe to say 'Scandinavian' for setts of the general colour and texture seen here, possibly recognising that the dull red Bohuslan Granite from Gothenburg may be amongst the rock types involved. Safer and more easy to identify are the several rock types used by Barry in his restoration of the Eleanor Cross in 1863. All are recognisable British rocks, beginning with the medium-grained grey granite which forms the base steps, and the foot of the cross. Badly flaked by rising damp and frost action, the roughened surfaces glint with the flakes of muscovite mica. The remainder of the rock is an even mosaic of grey or white feldspar, with darker, translucent quartz. Above this base are blocks of Portland Stone, including some on the west face (towards Trafalgar Square) which are very shelly, the fossils emerging due to weathering over the years. The upright shaft of the Cross involves a pale red sandstone (probably New Red Sandstone from Mansfield, Nottinghamshire) which has also weathered to a considerable extent. In part, this could be a reaction between porous and water-permeable rock (the limestone), the two thrown into direct contact by the design of the monument. The same juxtaposition of stones is often responsible for the flaking and premature decay of sandstone steps and flagging at the entrances of new buildings within a disappointingly short period of their completion. It would seem that people have forgotten the principles of damp coursing, or the effects of the differences in porosity between certain popular building stones.

The rebuilding of the decayed parts of Craven Street and Northumberland Street (1984), brings a natural halt to our progress towards Trafalgar Square, but this is convenient. Facing us is the blanker walling of South Africa House, which in all respects speaks only to Trafalgar Square, but that is the beginning of another walk.

*St Martin in the Fields, fountains in foreground, Scottish Granites*

# TRAFALGAR SQUARE AND
# ST. JAMES'S

In his book *The Necessary Monument*, Theo Crosby talks of the question of identity of cities as they are rebuilt and change from their former shape and architecture. Amongst the points which he makes is the observation that as new buildings replace old, there is the anger that they will all be good-of-their-kind, but by the same token, identical except in minor details. In this way, city-dwellers become inured to a uniformity, and may not 'identify' as they once did with place. In London, Trafalgar Square is the antithesis, in that its shape and the buildings which surround it are thoroughly familiar in most people's minds even though they have not visited it in the flesh, simply because it has figured in many public celebrations over the years. Victories, celebrations at Christmas, demonstrations of one kind or another, all have been filmed or televised so that the Square has become a natural focus for the capital as nowhere else. For our purpose too, it has potential, and is a splendid starting point, even though there are times when it is awkward, indeed hardly possible to stand and stare, let alone take out a hand-lens to distinguish between Scottish granites.

Assuming that we have found a quiet corner, we can begin with a broad sweep of the surrounding buildings, sensing the changes in style and building materials, beginning at the northeast corner with **St Martin in the Fields**.

Here we have yet another memorable spire fronting and capping a Portland Stone church of the late 18th century. Well outside the limits of the Great Fire of 1666, St Martin's has been shaken and begrimed by traffic for two centuries, and has become something of a test case for cleaning techniques in recent years. To the right and slightly downslope, **South Africa House** stands as one of those buildings of the thirties in which solid blocks of the same Portland Stone seem to grow whiter and whiter with the passage of time rather than becoming an anonymous grey. The marked contrast comes at the end of the Strand and Northumberland Avenue, where late 19th century buildings introduce pale brown oolitic limestone and facings of red granites. **Grand Buildings** to the north, and **Trafalgar Buildings** to the south, have both been under some threat of redevelopment, but survive if only to maintain a familiar roofline and frontage which completes the Square to the south and the approach to Whitehall—one of the great views of central London. Directly to the south, from the Admiralty Arch round into Cockspur Street, predominantly Edwardian buildings of a diversity of styles and rock types catch our attention, until we come to the solid and classical lines of **Canada House**, its Bath Stone bright and resplendent after recent cleaning. The northwest corner has been for so long an open space that whatever fills it as the extension to the National Gallery will be something of an intrusion, without even the promise of natural stone. It may, however, do something to help the proportions of the **National Gallery**, countering the balance given by St Martin's to the east. What would be unfortunate would be if the new building were to distract from the present focus of the Square, **Nelson's Column.** At present no disruptive modern building breaks into the panorama which we have just reviewed.

The large open space of Trafalgar Square, as it was named in 1820, was part of the grand design of John Nash, clearing away a confusion of low-grade dwellings and the Royal Mews, and opening up views of St Martin-in-the-Fields from the south for the first time. Geologically, the ground beneath the Square is part of the Thames Terrace sequence, the south face of the Taplow Terrace forming here a decided slope from the foot of Charing Cross Road to a 'cliff' in front of the National Gallery—the Square itself having been completely levelled by the later work of Barry. The tons of sand and silt removed at this time must have contained a rich fauna of bones and shells of an Ice Age interglacial period (the Ipswichian), which can now only be obtained in smaller temporary exposures when some building is enlarged or demolished and the site redeveloped. The deposit is famous for the bones of *Hippopotamus*, which testifies that 100,000 years before the present, the Thames was both warmer and extended further into the heart of the capital.

The focal point of the Square, **Nelson's Column** (**1**), was raised in 1842, some eight years after that commemorating the Duke of York on Carlton House Terrace, but honour was satisfied in its greater height (142' compared with 102' for the Duke). Designed by William Railton, the column is of massive drum sections of grey Fogginter Granite from Dartmoor, but there is little chance to make out its even-grained texture in the fine-axed surface finish to these surfaces. It is also difficult to confirm the precise location of Aberdeenshire Dancing Cairns Granite (Elsden & Howe, 1923), although this medium-grained, blue-grey granite, paler in tone than Rubislaw Granite, may be the rock of the recently cleaned bollards of the north side terrace facing the National Gallery. The dark variety of Peterhead Granite, Cairngall, has been mentioned as occurring in the base of the fountains, but only those brave enough to paddle in could verify this point. After so much uncertainty, it at least seems clear that the plinth to the Napier statue in the southwest corner of the Square is of granite from Lamorna Quarry near Penzance, a point proved by the clear presence of cruciform-twin crystals of orthoclase feldspar visible on the west face of the block, opposite Canada House.

Leaving the granites, the flagstones of the Square are a study in themselves for the sedimentary structures which they display through foot-tread wear over the century. A first point to note is their enormous size as paving slabs, suggesting that they came from the large flagstone quarries of the north of England and in all probability from the Coal Measures. With the passage of time, their original matt surfaces have become polished and worn down in places so as to breach a lower bedding level in the slab. In this way there has developed the fine black ring-marking of the surfaces as the fine lamination of the flagstone, picked out by mica and carbon flakes, is exposed. More expressive must be the delicate ripple-mark which has emerged through the same process in many of the slabs—a structure which is readily recognisable as the record of wind-ruffled waters of the Carboniferous sea shore, 250 million years before present. The pavement opposite South Africa House is particularly good for these structures, but there are many examples all around.

Yet more sedimentary structures are to be seen when we move up on to the northern terrace opposite the National Gallery and walk across the red and white chequer-board surface. The white squares are of Portland Stone, but a variety which is quite rich in shells of Jurassic oysters which weather back much less quickly than the surrounding stone so they stand up proud from the surface. On many of the same slabs, you can pick out strap-like markings

*National Gallery and St Martin in the Fields* (**2:3**)

*Portico and Royal Arms, St. Martin in the Fields (3)*

sometimes arranged in hexagons, which are trails and shallow burrows created by mud-eating organisms when the lime sediment was still soft. These are trace-fossils, not so much fossils in themselves but rather a preservation of the activities of fossils which are not now preserved for us to see. Turning now to the red squares, these are of New Red Sandstone from the quarries of Mansfield, a stone which clearly has weathered more quickly under foot-tread than the adjacent limestone. Some of the sandstone flags show a banding across their surfaces which suggests that the slabs were weakly current-bedded. While we might be critical of the choice of stone in this terrace, there is no doubt about the visual success of the multi-colour pattern as we look towards St Martin in the one direction and Canada House in the other.

There is little to be said about the **National Gallery** (**2**); it is of Portland Stone, including the columns to the portico which were salvaged from an earlier building on Carlton House Terrace, demolished in 1829. The Gallery has been the subject of criticism for its long low profile and its oddly proportioned drum-based

central dome. Added to all this, there are the small pepper-pot towers at either end which have led Summerson to refer to the skyline as 'like the clock and vases on a mantelpiece, only less useful'. William Wilkins, the architect, completed the Gallery between 1832 and 1838, some years after he had got the proportions right for a similar classical portico and dome at University College in Gower Street (1827–29). Perhaps the stretched lateral scale of the Trafalgar Square site was sufficient to destroy the composition.

Moving to **St Martin-in-the-Fields** (**3**), we have a church which was rebuilt by James Gibbs between 1722 and 1726, when the treatment was to give a skin of Portland Stone to an older structure. We have well-worn 18th century Upper Jurassic limestone for everyone to see at their leisure on the broad steps of the Portico, which is so convenient a resting place through the summer months of the year. While it could be said that little changes, the walls behind us are something of a history of the stone-cleaning movement, having first been tackled by dry sand-blasting in 1967–68, then a second time in 1970–71 because of a patchy effect from the first effort, this in turn to be followed by some washing and brushing (1979–80) in the manner which would be standard for the cleaning of limestone buildings today. What we would also recognise now is the fact that buildings of this age will always be liable to colour contrasts, however successful a cleaning operation may have been. This reflects a natural weathering on exposure to local microclimates, and different degrees of penetration by grime and pollutants on exposed faces.

**South Africa House** (4) is a solid Portland Stone building, representing good quality Whit-Bed of the 1930's, weathered over some fifty years. The small touches of decoration are sufficient to identify it as South African—the lion and antelope heads to the keystones of the first floor and the Dutch East Indiaman sailing ship of the high pediment. South Africa House maintains a kind of Imperial tradition in style and solidity and was the work of Sir Herbert Baker, sometime architect to the Governments of India, Kenya and South Africa.

Southwards across the Strand, we come to the first of two blunt-nosed buildings which rise on either side of Northumberland Avenue. The first is **Grand Buildings** (5), the second on the south side is **Trafalgar Buildings** (6). In the past, both have been cluttered by scaffolding and signs in their upper floors, and much of our attention may have been drawn by the shops and boutiques which sprout at pavement level. These are, however, recent uses for what were designed as Victorian 'Grand Hotels', purpose-built between 1880 and 1882 at strategic locations by the architects the Francis Brothers. Both have upper walling of yellow-brown Bath Stone, with columns, swags and urns of the same material, but in the case of Trafalgar Buildings (the old Trafalgar Hotel) there are columns of New Red Sandstone attached to the first and second floors. It is at pavement level that variety of stone increases, involving some of the original facings to the Hotel, and some much later shop-fitting adventures. In Grand Buildings there survive from the 1880's, columns and shafts of pink Peterhead Granite. In Trafalgar Buildings opposite, the pink granite is associated with a deeper red rock which is Corennie Granite from Alford, Aberdeenshire (seen in the Chemists shop entrance), and a very rich red granite which is Swedish Imperial Red Granite, identified by its crushed feldspar crystals. For good measure, there are also touches of Finnish Baltic Brown Granite to be seen in the main entrance to the Buildings, off Northumberland Avenue.

To emphasise that this was considered to be the prime area for Hotels in late Victorian times, the overwhelming mass of what was the **Victoria Hotel** follows on in sequence along Northumberland Avenue (7) of Portland Stone, and to a very French Imperial style, our interest could be the decidedly yellow

*South Africa House, Trafalgar Square* (4)

*Grand Buildings, Trafalgar Square (5)*

surface of the southern end of the building, where recent cleaning has rendered the Portland surfaces almost as brown as Bath Stone (to be seen in the fabric of the **Metropole** (**8**) a little further down the street).

Altogether, Northumberland Avenue can be overpowering in the scale of its buildings, making it a relief to escape to the diversity of the southern side of Trafalgar Square once more, where we return to Drummond's Bank of the **Royal Bank of Scotland** (**9**). It stands at the head of Whitehall and on the corner leading to Admiralty Arch and the Mall, with several points of geological interest. First, it is one of those sites which in the past has seen foundation work breaking into the shell and bone deposits of the Trafalgar Square Interglacial period, and at one time, bones of ox, lion and elephant are said to have been proudly preserved in the bank itself (Fletcher, 1981). The second point brings us to the building itself, which is of Portland Stone, recently cleaned, but with additions of red sandstone in panels and pillars to the entrance, giving a strong colour contrast. The sandstone shows a delicate pattern of ripple-drift as it has weathered on site, and has a darker colour than that normally associated with New Red Sandstone from Mansfield. For this reason, it is possible that it might be one of the red sandstones from Dumfriesshire or Ayrshire which make such a contribution to the sandstone buildings

of Glasgow. Here in London, the stone as it has been used has tended to crumble and decay, and the restoration work has included a painting of the surfaces most affected with a red stone-textured paint. A final point about this bank must be to draw attention to its drive-in cash point facing on to the Mall. Not only is this something novel in British banks, but this example of an American service has seen the introduction of some splendid surfaces of Belgian Bleu Belge Marble in the supporting pillars to the canopy and to the troughs which contain the flower displays. The marble is black rather than blue, and is crossed by a regular pattern of tension veins of white calcite. Its Carboniferous age is demonstrated by one or two slabs which bear clisiophyllid corals in addition to the customary small crinoid ossicles.

Crossing the Mall, we come to a range of premises with contrasting styles and varied building stones. On the corner is **Uganda House** (**10**), of rather sombre 'black granite', brownish in tone rather than the customary intense black, possibly from a rusty weathering of the included pyrite minerals. Next door, the **Bristol & West Building Society** (**11**) is a small neat office with bow windows and details, all in yellowed Portland Stone, which would have been at home in Cheapside or the City. At ground floor level, the interior has been modernised by the introduction of rough riven slabs of dark grey slate which may be either

*The National Westminster Bank, Trafalgar Square (**13**)*

Burlington Slate from the Lake District, or Dinorwic Slate from North Wales. With the **Canadian Pacific Office** next door (**12**), we return to the grand scale of buildings which seek to impose a presence and at the same time advertise their purpose to the passing public. Here it was done with stone medallions high up on the facade, depicting a transatlantic liner of 1903, a genuine Canadian locomotive with cowcatcher and bell, and beavers and sheaves of corn—all done in Portland Stone. At ground floor and extending up to first floor, the walls are of heavily rusticated, fine-axed grey granite, with the entrance flanked by silver-grey larvikite married with deep red Swedish Balmoral Granite, the whole effect being very modern. This scale and richness of colour is offset by the simplicity of the **National Westminster Bank** (**13**), built originally as a branch of the National Provincial Bank in 1871. This building shares some of the elegance of all the branches of that Victorian bank, notably those seen in Bishopsgate and in Chancery Lane. In Trafalgar Square, the bank was the work of F. W. Porter, and involves rusticated Portland Stone above a base of axe-finished grey granite, with the most striking detail being the tall polished columns of pink Peterhead Granite which add rich colour to the

design. Seen from across the Square, equally striking are the tall stove-pipe chimneys of gleaming white Portland Stone.

Facing us across Cockspur Street is **Canada House** (**14**), recently cleaned, fronted on this side by an imposing entrance flanked by massive columns topped by Ionic capitals. Canada House has grown around a core which was the Royal College of Physicians building, designed by Smirke in 1824. As that building was of Bath Stone, the same material was used for the extensions to the south and west, with touches of white Portland limestone adding colour contrast. It is here that we can best study the rock which is less accessible in the old hotels of Northumberland Avenue, noting in particular the strongly-bedded shelly variety of Bath Stone, sometimes mistaken as 'ragstone' because of its rough, grainy texture compared with the usual freestone qualities for which the rock type is famous. Wear and tear, followed by patching of one kind or another, are all features which we can see on the surfaces of this building.

Geological walks in town invariably involve much crossing and recrossing of streets as a building catches the eye; so it is with Cockspur Street where, as often is the case, older buildings have received a face-

*Canada House,*
*Cockspur Street* (**14**)

lift at pavement level. In the case of No. 28, the upper floors seen from the north pavement are heavy with terracotta mouldings attached to a brick frontage, with panels depicting Atlas bearing the World on his shoulders, or just a Globe itself. These details are another example of Doulton Ware, fashioned especially for the original premises of Stanfords, for so long the source of maps and globes in London.

Equally identifiable from the symbols and motifs it bears would be **Norway House** (**15**), with St Olav in a niche above an entrance flanked by arms and shields of Viking and Norwegian character. What would not be so easy to determine, if it were not recorded, is the fact that the grey granite of the ground floor and entrance is Iddefjord Granite from the eastern side of Oslo Fjord close to Fredrikstad and the Swedish border. Once again, the difficulty lies in the fact that the stone is here axe-dressed and not polished so as to show clearly its texture and mineral composition. Following this showing of the flag at pavement level,

Norway House accepts British Portland Stone for its upper floors.

Scandinavian stone returns, however, in the **Bureau de Change** (**16**), once the premises of the French Lines when Transatlantic crossings were made by sea in liners such as the *Normandie*. The chateau-shape of this building is supported by squared pillars of Swedish Virgo Granite (identified by its violet-blue quartz crystals), the deep red colour offset by blocks of silver-grey larvikite. In the modern refitting of the banking hall, the flooring has been replaced by slabs of brown Italian Perlato Marble, rich in fossils including bryozoa, algae and broken shells of bivalves, all of Cretaceous age.

For the buildings which follow, the **Scottish Centre** (**17**) and the **Greyhound Bus Company** (**18**), it is the view from the opposite pavement which tells all. The Scottish Centre was originally the headquarters of Canadian National Railways, the arch rivals of the C.P.R. further down the street, and their national pride is expressed in the arms of the

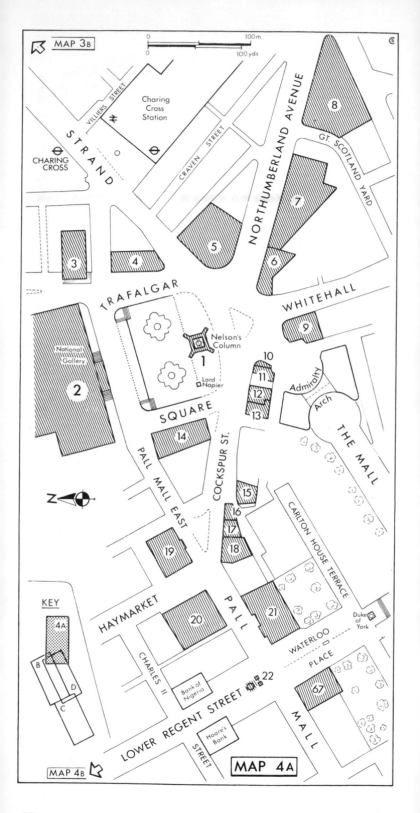

*New Zealand House,
Cockspur Street (20)*

provinces carved in the Portland Stone of the upper floors. Next door is a little more exotic, having originally been built in 1907 for Peninsular & Orient Lines which goes some way to explaining the decoration to the upper floors, the granite cupola and the capping golden ship weathervane. Larvikite and a fine-axed grey granite of uncertain source are the stones involved here. We are now at the corner of Cockspur Street with Pall Mall, and this is the viewpoint from which to look at one of the most French-looking buildings in London, **Kinnaird House (19)**, now a computer centre for Barclays Bank. The building was completed in 1922 to the design of the architect Blomfield who was responsible for much that stands in Piccadilly Circus today, often with style and detail which are evident here. The use of strongly rusticated Portland Stone is one shared character; steeply pitched mansard roofs and bull's eye windows are another. What is striking about Kinnaird House, however, is the soaring verticals of the design, coupled with two of the tallest end-towers imaginable, as well as the high quality of the Portland Stone after cleaning.

Looking across to the opposite corner of Haymarket, there stands the tower of **New Zealand House (20)**, a very tall glass-encased block of some fifteen floors, which is surprisingly unobtrusive in the local townscape. Geologically, it is the large stalk-base to the tower which draws our attention, a happier situation than having to peer upwards to unattainable heights to try to identify a token stone detail. At pavement level are extensive panels of Carboniferous Limestone, as black and dense as some slates, but recognisable from the tiny crinoid ossicles which are sprinkled across the polished surfaces. More diagnostic still, are the small zaphrentid corals, and the white shell cross-sections of the brachiopods *Productus* and *Spirifer*, which need to be searched for, a procedure which always attracts attention from passers-by. As a rock type, it could have come from west of Ireland, the north of England, but very probably came from the black limestone quarries of Tournai in Belgium. While provenance is a problem, we can rest content with the identification as limestone.

Moving west along Pall Mall, we can take in a classical club, **The**

*Kinnaird House, Pall Mall East (19)*

**Institute of Directors** (formerly the United Services Club) (**21**). This building has had a complex history starting with a Smirke core, modified by Nash, and finally given its present form including the relief frieze, by Decimus Burton. While it contributes nothing geologically to the scene (brick overlain by stucco rendering), it does much to give character and atmosphere to Waterloo Place and this part of Pall Mall. From this point we can appreciate the symmetrically planned series of grand banks and offices, all of Portland Stone and all conforming in style, which give a harmony to Lower Regent Street as it rises smoothly to Piccadilly. **Hoare's Bank** and **Trafalgar House** make up the west wall; **Lloyds Bank** and the **Bank of Nigeria** the eastern mirror-image. All units have massive columns, equally massive capitals and decorated cornices. All units are singularly free from colour contrasts which might have sprung from the use of granites to offset the grey-whiteness of Portland limestone. For granites, we have to look to the **Crimean War Memorial** (**22**), which stands in a focal position just to the north of the Pall Mall crossing.

In fact it is The Guard's Memorial, with bronze Grenadiers, Coldstreamers and Fusiliers standing on a rough-axed plinth of grey, large-feldspar granite which could be De Lank Granite from Bodmin Moor, Cornwall. The upper part of the plinth is Cheeswring Granite, also from that same part of the county. In both cases, the rough surface finish hinders direct assessments. This is no problem in the nearby statues of Florence Nightingale and Sydney Herbert (the Secretary for War who supported her in her work in the hospital at Scutari). Both stand on plinths of pink Peterhead Granite, which in turn stand upon bases of pale grey granite with visible crystals of pink feldspar, which hint that this too may be a Peterhead Granite. The monument is a safe place from which to take in one of the grander elements of London town planning, albeit work of nearly two centuries ago—the Nash plan for Lower Regent Street and Piccadilly. Geologically, the smooth rise represents a climb across the surface of the same terrace face which we mentioned in Trafalgar Square, reaching the higher level of the Taplow Terrace in Piccadilly. Having taken this into account, there is relatively little else to claim

80

*The Crimean War Memorial, Waterloo Place (**22**)*

our attention until we reach Piccadilly, or rather Jermyn Street. The latter is an outer ripple of the plan of the first decade of this century which almost achieved what has proved impossible ever since, the completion of an acceptable scheme of buildings for Piccadilly Circus. What we see from Jermyn Street are two massive and complementary units, **Barclays Bank** on the west side (**23**), **Lillywhites** on the east (**24**), in which solid Portland Stone is dressed and rusticated in such a fashion that you could well have believed that granite was involved. Both the style and the treatment were an essential part of Blomfield's plan for both the Circus and for Regent Street, parts of which were implemented between 1910 and 1930, but at that point, were left incomplete on the north and northeast quarters. Blomfield's task was to harmonise, under the scrutiny of the Crown Commissioners, the curving Quadrant of Regent's Street, the enormous new Piccadilly Hotel of Norman Shaw, and his own new buildings which were to replace a confusion of late-Victorian premises of varying architectural worth. A key building in the new structure, was the New County Fire Office, which in 1927 became the present **Sun Alliance Building** (**25**), deeply arcaded at pavement level and topped by a flat profile dome and a statue of Britannia. With the heavy rustication of the Portland Stone once again, including the radiating pattern which emphasises the arcading, this building occupies a focal position in views of the Circus from the south and east, and deserves better support from the Monico and Pavillion sites. To the west, such support is given by the once-**Swan & Edgar's** building (**26**), which repeats the use of Portland Stone in massive block units, and repeats the rustication which simply adds to that sense of solid mass. Piccadilly Circus is not the best place for casual geology, but it is worthwhile peering into the entrance to **The Clydesdale Bank** in the southwest corner for sight of the interior walling of brecciated white Arebescato Marble quarried from the Lucca district south of Carrara. The white Jurassic limestone has been broken into large fragments separated by wisps of grey clay.

When we move westwards along Piccadilly, there are marked contrasts between north and south pavements. The north, the sunny side, carries on from Swan & Edgar's in height, mass and the same white Portland Stone. The south side is very much more varied in all respects, including the use of the buildings. For example, No. 212 Piccadilly, now a **Saxone** shop (**27**), was once a National Provincial Bank designed by the architect Gibson. If we stand back and look above the heavy pebble-dash of the ground floor, we can note the attached columns and window surrounds, but particularly the heavy cornice at roof level, supported by dragons with outspread wings. Another branch of The National Provincial Bank, now the **National Westminster,** stands

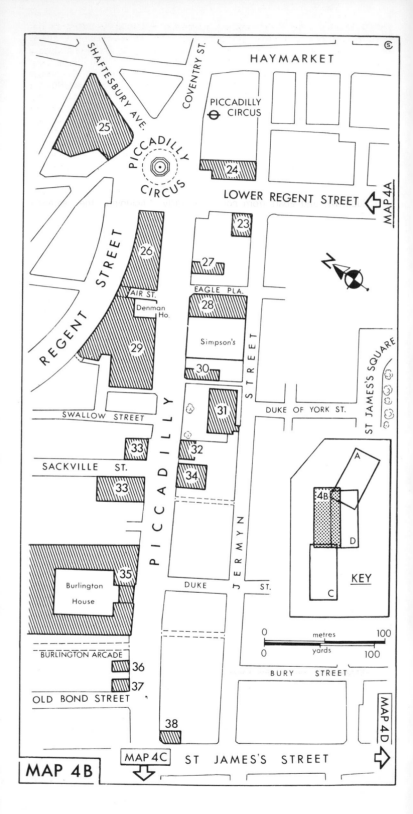

MAP 4B

a short distance away at the head of Eagle Place (**28**), still bearing the medallion coat of arms of the older bank above the corner entrance. The bank was designed by Alfred Waterhouse (1894) and built in Portland Stone without any hint of his favourite red-brick and fiery red terracotta of High Holborn and The Prudential commissions. The Portland is offset by the introduction of polished round columns of grey, oatmeal-speckled Kemnay Granite from mid-Aberdeenshire. This granite is of a much lighter grey colour than Rubislaw, and apart from colour, has significantly higher proportions of silvery muscovite mica glinting from its surfaces. The interior marble is splendid, including both Ashburton and the pale buff Petitor Marbles from Devon.

This point on the southern pavement is probably the best position from which to view the imposing mass of the Piccadilly Hotel to the north, but we might well begin with an elegant neighbour of very different character. **Denman House**, squeezed between the Hotel and Swan & Edgar's, is a highly decorated set of chambers with shops at pavement level. The decoration begins with a full-relief coat of arms above the entrance to Cordings the Outfitters, and continuing in bands of vigorously realistic foliage at several levels across the frontage. There are vine leaves and grapes at first floor, curling tendrils and fronds at the second, and groupings of sinuous carp at third floor balcony level. In all,

Denman House is yet another demonstration, if we needed it, of the potential of good freestone quality Portland Stone in the hands of a monumental mason with free scope. Built in 1903, a date worked into the detail of the ornamentation, this building was here two years before Norman Shaw began his **Piccadilly Hotel** next door (**29**) and proceeded to raise the skyline of Piccadilly by some four or five storeys. Shaw's hotel was originally intended to take in the total restructuring of the southern end of Regent's Street and Piccadilly, including the arcaded Quadrant of John Nash, but this was not completed before his death (1907), when Blomfield took over the plan for Regent's Street and completed it to his own design. As it is, the Piccadilly frontage to the Hotel can sometimes give the impression of being incomplete in that while there is a tall gable to the west end of the colonnade screen, there is nothing to balance it to the east. The most striking feature of the building is the heavy rock-faced finish given to the Portland Stone blocks which have the effect of giving Piranesian mass to the Hotel—a ground floor effect sustained upwards by the rustication of the surface. It was this aspect of style which Blomfield borrowed and extended into his later buildings which surround the Circus, so giving a harmony to the whole area as far as it was completed.

On the south side of Piccadilly, beyond Simpson's, the **Bank of Credit & Commerce (30)**, offers two

*Burlington House (centre left) and Piccadilly*

red granites, the deeper red being Swedish Imperial Red, while the more numerous pale red pillars are of Peterhead Granite. Although we have seen these same rock types several times already, these 'outcrops' are noteworthy for their condition. However durable and lasting igneous rocks may be in buildings, it is still necessary to maintain their effect by periodic cleaning and resurfacing even if it is only a washing from time to time.

At this point, Piccadilly widens as we come to the churchyard of **St James' Piccadilly** (**31**), a Wren church with some similarity to St Andrew Holborn in its simple design, and built of dull red brick with white stone dressings. The west tower is capped by another interesting Wren steeple which looks convincingly lead-covered, but which is of lighter and more serviceable fibreglass in fact.

In the western corner of the paved yard, the **Midland Bank** of Edwin Lutyens, 1922, stands as an acceptable chapel to Mammon (**32**), if only for the high-quality rubbed red brick and the bricklaying skill demonstrated in details such as the shallow niche on the street wall. It is all very neat and clean-lined when compared with the massive and ornate twin buildings, **Lloyds Bank** and the **Italian Trade Centre** which stand at the foot of Sackville Street opposite (**33**). Both are of creamy-white Portland Stone of Whit-Bed quality, enhanced in the bank by black-painted metalwork and gilded wreaths. Older Portland Stone is to be seen in the strangely blank-walled Piccadilly front to the **Royal Institute of Painters in Watercolour** (**34**), a building of 1831, whose ground floor is borrowed by Panam Airline. Where windows might have been, there are shallow niches occupied by the busts of watercolourists who, apart from Turner and Girtin, must now tax our powers of recognition. This and other buildings which quickly follow as we move along Piccadilly serve as case studies in the programme of cleaning of buildings which has run its course over the past ten years. Some have clearly been improved, while others may have suffered from loss of surface. Most if not all are of Portland Stone, so comparisons are reasonable to draw. The judgement must be personal, and is left to you, but anyone could be forgiven if they took the stone of the vaulted entr-

ance to the courtyard of **Burlington House** as being Millstone Grit or some similar coarse-grained sandstone. It is instead rather flayed and blasted Portland Stone of yellowish hue (**35**).

All this uniformity changes when we pass beyond the painted elegance of The Burlington Arcade and come to **Colette House** (**36**). Here, the deep-set rounded arches are lined by a deep red Scandinavian granite in which the large red feldspar crystals have been visibly crushed by deformation post-dating crystallisation. This rock would be one of the 'older' granites of the Swedish or Finnish Caledonian Shield of the Baltic. Colette House was refitted in 1975 by Ronald Ward and Partners, who added an interesting intermixture of scored tiles to the pre-existing red and yellow sandstones of the upper floors to give an overall Middle Eastern character to the frontage. As it happens, the prevailing red colour of Colette House blends quite naturally with the premises next door, the Jewellers **Tyme** on the corner of Bond Street (**37**). They have some of the most impressive looking surfaces of Shap Granite that you can see anywhere in London in their ground floor. The large buff-coloured orthoclase crystals stand out quite clearly against a rather deep brown background to illustrate for us the texture of a true Porphyry, and once again it seems worth saying that here we have another example of the stunning effect of good natural stone in buildings when it is well-maintained.

From this high watermark in Bond Street, the office of the **Norwich Union Insurance** (**38**) at the head of St James's Street could look just 'ordinary' with its slightly washed-out pink stone combined with what looks like grey Portland Stone at a higher level. In fact it is a unique building involving a most unlikely material, Precambrian Jasper from the Lleyn Peninsula in North Wales. This was recorded by Elsden in his book on London building stones (1923), but came to light afresh recently when the repair work was described in *Stone Industries* (Burton, 1980). The work involved the taking down of facing blocks which had suffered cracking and their trimming and slicing into cladding panels which could then be reattached to the building as sound stone. Why this was necessary relates to the

Norwich Union Insur-
ance, St Jame's Street
(**38**)

Jasper in the door-
case, St Jame's
Street (**38**)

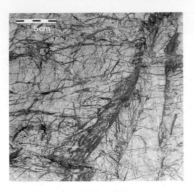

*Jasper* (**38**)

virtual impossibility of quarrying fresh supplies of the same rock from the original workings near Aberdaron today. The extremely hard pink stone is a mixture of cryptocrystalline silica and dolomite which occurs as lens-form masses within the Gwna Volcanics of the Monian Series of Anglesey and Lleyn. Allowing for metal fatigue or rusting of the fixings, this stone should last forever, or at least longer than the associated Greek Pentelikon Marble which looks like grey Portland Stone. Pentelikon is a white or cream coloured marble with a faint blue or grey veining which emerges as fine dark lines crossing the surfaces on weathering. Quarried in the Marathon district of mid-Greece and widely used present-day, it is thought that this use in the Norwich Union office was one of the first introductions of the marble for external use in London (1905). A final note is to draw attention to the panels of bright red marble which underlie the ground floor windows. This is an example of a rudistid marble, thought to come from the Cretaceous limestones of Spain. The

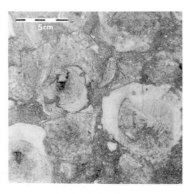

*Rudistid limestone*

rudists are thick-shelled bivalves, seen here as ring-shapes in creamy white calcite standing out boldly against the dull red background of lime mud—an excellent combination for judging a limestone as having 'marble quality'. Rudists are very much a feature of the Cretaceous rocks of southern Europe developed within the confines of the Tethys Ocean. For all these reasons—Jasper, Pentelikon and rudistid marble—we could very well ask that The Norwich Union office should be scheduled for preservation as a geological monument, if not on architectural grounds.

Having seen Pentelikon Marble, it is not such a problem to recognise it again when it occurs in the office of the **Bradford & Bingley Building Society** on the opposite side of St James' Street (**39**). The marble itself is best seen in the entrance pillars and steps leading from St James' Street (where it is No. 49) where curving and swirling patterns have emerged as the stone has weathered back from the original smooth-dressed surfaces. Otherwise, the building itself has several interesting architectural touches, including Art Nouveau details such as the attenuated figures which casually seem to support the upper floors with their arms folded above their heads.

If Pentelikon could have been mistaken for dirty Portland Stone in the buildings which we have just looked at, there could be no mistake about the real thing as seen in **Barclays Bank**, 157–160 Piccadilly (**40**). Above a token base of axe-dressed grey granite, the bank is of massive blocks of very white Whit- or Base-Bed Portland, including the fluted columns and hefty Corinthian capitals. In the affluent year when it was built (1922) the bank received an RIBA medal, no doubt for its marble-enriched and laquered interior as much as its external form which is at least in keeping with its neighbour, the **Ritz Hotel** just across Arlington Street (**41**).

For several reasons other than its unquestioned status as an hotel, The Ritz has considerable reputation. We have already seen some of the earliest custom-built hotels in Northumberland Avenue off Trafalgar Square, and can recognise that between 1880 and 1906 when The Ritz was completed, a total revolution had taken place in the increased size

*The Ritz Hotel, Piccadilly (**41**)*

of floors and room space, but especially in the provision of ground floor lounges, salons and dining rooms (Boniface, 1981). The Ritz was architect designed throughout by Mewès and Davis from its innovatory steel-framed core and its French external detail, through to the decoration and furnishing of its rooms. Geologically, the rather anonymous grey, axe-dressed granite of the street front arcading is the same Iddefjord Granite from Oslo Fjord which we have already seen in Norway House in Cockspur Street (**15** above).

The massive rounded arches of The Ritz have a pale reflection in the front of **Trafalgar House** opposite (**42**), a building of finely finished smooth Portland Stone. At pavement level, however, the squared pillars to the street are of a light brown granite thought to be Old Gold Granite from Brazil. Fine in grain, the rock is not obviously rich in free quartz and so is strictly not a true granite but rather a granodiorite or diorite. Leaving aside such niceties, as seen in the pillars to the Aeroflot Office, the 'granite' is shot through with slender veins of more finely crystalline material, from which in turn are developed colour rings pas-

sing out into the rock as a whole. This gives a clear impression of later alteration of the original rock, which was one of the intrusives of the Precambrian Shield of Brazil. Trafalgar House was completed in 1974 by Chapman, Taylor & Partners as a complex extending into both Berkeley and Dover Streets, where large surfaces of the Brazilian rock are available for study. Close to the Dover Street entrance stands Elizabeth Frink's statue 'Horse and Rider' mounted on a low plinth of very new Shap Granite, appreciably paler in colour than the rich brown variant seen at Tyme jewellers (see **37** above).

To the west, **Devonshire House** and **Stratton House** are twin cliffs of gleaming white Portland Stone with nothing to add by way of geological comment, so we shall pass on to Nos. **82–83 Piccadilly** where Portland Stone at the upper levels is set off by contrasting rock types at pavement level (**43**). In Reed International, for example, there are large cross walls to the entrance of South African Rustenberg Bon Accord Gabbro, one of the paler of the 'Black Granites' in popular use, the grey patches of plagioclase feldspar lightening up the overall

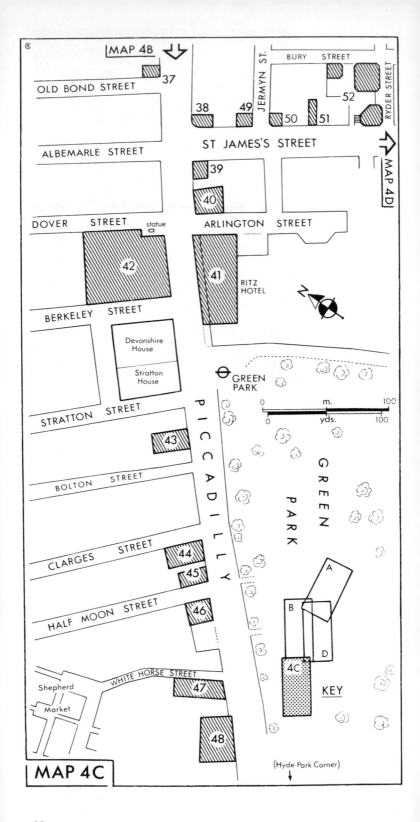

*No. 100 Piccadilly*
(**47**)

surfaces. Next door in the Xerox Office, pale blue larvikite is introduced to contrast with the dark grey Rustenberg Gabbro.

Diversity continues across Clarges Street at the Lebanese Restaurant *Fakhreldine* (**44**) in the intensely black sheet wall which bears the gilded sign. A close scrutiny of the smooth black surfaces will eventually reveal the presence of small white discs which are crinoid ossicles; to these can be added wispy cross-sections of thin-shelled brachiopods, and finally, faint strap-like markings which are the traces left by burrowing organisms as they ate the soft sediment. All builds up to the conclusion that this is a muddy Carboniferous Limestone, similar to that seen in New Zealand House in Cockspur Street (see **20** above).

Next door, in **Libyan Airways**, (**45**) we have a repeat of the red granite seen in Colette House (see **36** above), as you can prove by noting the crushed feldspar crystals. Looking through the large windows, you will notice that the window sills inside are faced with the black and white veined marble from the Meuse Valley known as Bleu Belge Marble (Groessens, 1981). Tracing the white veins and noticing their

regular offset across the slabs, you can appreciate that they relate to tension and fracture.

We now come to **91–93 Piccadilly**, which Pevsner notes as the last brick building of Piccadilly before the towering cliffs of Green Park. Of modest red brick with grey-painted terracotta mouldings, these shops and chambers are decorated with polished columns of dark coloured Shap Granite towards Piccadilly, and the sombre grey Irish granite, Bessbrook up the side street, all making a very typical package for 1883 (**46**).

As we come to the loftier buildings facing on to Green Park, **100 Piccadilly** is the first unit we meet beyond White Horse Street. It spent most of 1982 and much of 1983 shrouded in scaffolding as it was gutted and restored from within, leaving the external walling more-or-less intact. The interest to us of this building (**47**) lies in the fact that it involves the Jurassic Ham Hill Stone from the Yeovil district of Somerset. From the blocks seen in this building during the recent work, it was easy to appreciate that Ham Hill Stone is a strongly calcite-cemented bioclastic limestone showing cross-bedding and structures which are more typical of sandstones than of normal

*International Maritime Organisation, Green Park, (48)*

limestones. Some distinct bands were clearly weaker than the rest, their poorer cementation having been the cause of faster decay within the fabric. Proved to be an excellent stone in the clean air of the West Country, one has to have reservations about its worth in the polluted air of London.

We have now reached the natural boundary of the Tyburn Stream, responsible for the marked down-dip in the road in front of us, but are drawn on by the geology of Nos. 101–102, the **International Maritime Organisation** (**48**). Here we have large polished columns of dark Shap Granite attached to the frontage and extending to the second floor in unbroken lengths which must be close to the practical limit for stone turning. While this is a point to savour, yet another geological fact remains to be noted. Behind the columns, the slightly grimy blocks of the main walling do not look anything special, and once again, could be passed off as 'dirty Portland' without a second glance. The rock is, however, figured and crossed by wispy dark lines which might hint at their being fine white sandstone. In fact, the rock is White Salten Marble from Norway which,

when fresh, has a slightly pinkish flush to it. Once again, it is Elsden in his book who offers this information, together with two further points. The first is that when the building was completed for the Junior Constitutional Club in 1890, it was the first building in London to be fitted with marble as external walling. The second fact he offers is to the effect that during the First World War, the building had its conspicuous whiteness dulled with grey camouflage paint which still clings to the surface with such sad effect (Elsden, 1923).

From this point we need to retrace our steps to St James's Street, conveniently following the southern pavement to be able to observe from a distance the buildings which we have already studied at close quarters. When we reach St James's Street, we can begin our study with **Connaught House** on the corner of Jermyn Street (**49**), another elegant branch of The National Westminster Bank. This is an Edwardian building with bulging bow-windows and balconies in cleaned white Portland Stone, set off by the polished rounded columns of oatmeal speckled Kemnay Granite from mid-Aberdeenshire. We could at this point divert along Jermyn Street if

*Connaught House, St James's Street* **(49)**

only to take in some of the opulent new marble facings which some of the shops of quality have acquired in recent years. Instead, we will continue down St James's Street, but taking in the broad frontage of **Davidoff** (**50**), not only the source of a good Havana cigar, but also a splendid exposure of Italian Arebescato Marble from the southern part of the Carrara region. It needs but little imagination to 'read' the pattern of events, the physical break up of a limestone followed by its reconstitution as a limestone breccia at the end of the deformation. A true marble.

'Black Granite' of a dense black tone, crowded with metallic minerals is to be seen in both the **Abbey National Office** and the **Clydesdale Bank** next door, but both are overshadowed by the full use of deep-red Swedish Virgo Granite in the entire ground floor frontage to **William Tilman** Antiques and the Chemists next door (**51**). The granite shows the physical breakdown of the feldspars and, in the door posts, the violet coloured quartz crystals which characterise it.

Boodles Club remains geologically anonymous, but this is not the case with what follows—the redeveloped

**Economist** site (**52**) set back from the line of the street as three separate towers linked by a raised paved area reached by a broad flight of steps. To quote one of several comments on the architectural merit involved, it has been said that 'this was one of the first modern buildings which has enhanced rather than destroyed the character of the area in which it was built. . .' (McKean & Jestico, 1976).

We can applaud this work of the architects Alison and Peter Smithson in that they chose to use Portland Roach as the stone facings to the towers and for the paved area and steps. It was roughly in 1964 that Roach began to appear in buildings as architects came to appreciate the interesting textures and tones which the cavity-rich limestone offered in contrast to smooth ashlar finished stone or vast areas of window glass. We can have a field day on the ramp surfaces and balustrades away from the busy pavements, 'discovering' the typical Portland fossils. What makes these slabs particularly interesting, however, is that they represent a half-way stage between the tight-locked texture of normal Portland Stone and the thoroughly leached Roach in which all the

*The Economist Office, St James's Street (**52**)*

original shell of fossils has been destroyed by groundwater solution. Many of the shells actually stand up proudly and positively instead of being subdued in the normal way.

Ryder Street brings us to the northern face of the massive block of St James's House, shared between the **Dunlop Rubber Company** and **Lloyds Bank** (**53**). In style, the Portland Stone is rock-faced after the pattern which we have already seen in Piccadilly Circus, but there the comparison ends. As was the case for many Edwardian banks, Lloyds banking hall is lined with yellow and buff marbles, colours which often seem to come from Apennine Italy close to Siena. South of King Street, much of the character of the 'townscape' of St James's Street stems from the painted woodwork and old glass of period shops—nice, but devoid of stone. In these circumstances we shift our attention to the opposite side of the street to the former **Conservative Club** (**54**).

This building must represent what

*Detail of Portland Roach Limestone (**52**)*

*Mark Mason's Hall,
St James's Street*
(**55**)

must be in everyone's mind when the word 'Club' is mentioned. It is massive in scale, with large attached columns, tall pedimented windows and completely lacking means of identification. Even today when it is no longer a Club, the front only bears the number '74'. All is in Portland Stone, slightly yellowed and dingy, but this only serves to set off the unique palace next door (**55**). This was built in 1862 as the Thatched House Club to the design of Knowles. Now **Mark Mason's Hall**, the remarkable feature is the use of Bath Stone in conjunction with some white Portland Stone, with the extensive development of in-depth sculptural decoration in the orange brown oolite. Between the windows at all floors there climb, one could almost say 'grow', stems of fully leaved ivy (central positions) or oak (either side of the door). What is more, in the roundels at the top of each floor, and on the spandrels of the arches, this thicket of foliage supports bird's nests with a wide range of birds, some alighting, some roosting to the indifference of live pigeons. No building could so fully demonstrate the good 'freestone' quality of this Middle Jurassic oolitic limestone.

Next door, is a gleaming white building of recently cleaned Portland Stone (**56**) a branch of the **Sun Alliance Assurance** designed by Norman Shaw (1904–05). This can explain the bold arches and the strong rustication of the ground and first floors if we cast our mind back to his work in the Piccadilly Hotel of about the same time. Here there is more delicacy in that the Portland Stone has a smooth ashlar finish and none of the rock-faced chiselling which give added mass to the hotel. The curious fact is that the same architect some twenty years earlier (1883), had completed a building for the same company on the opposite side of the street. Nothing could be more different from the Portland Stone office with its clean-lined front than the Dutch-gabled building on the opposite corner of Pall Mall (**57**)—a building which is seldom seen as fast moving traffic negotiates the tight corner into St James's Street three abreast. If you stop, however, and view from either Marlborough House or the Post Office tucked into the corner of No. 88, you will see a building which used very typical late-Victorian materials—fiery red brick combined with Portland Stone dressings. Special Norman

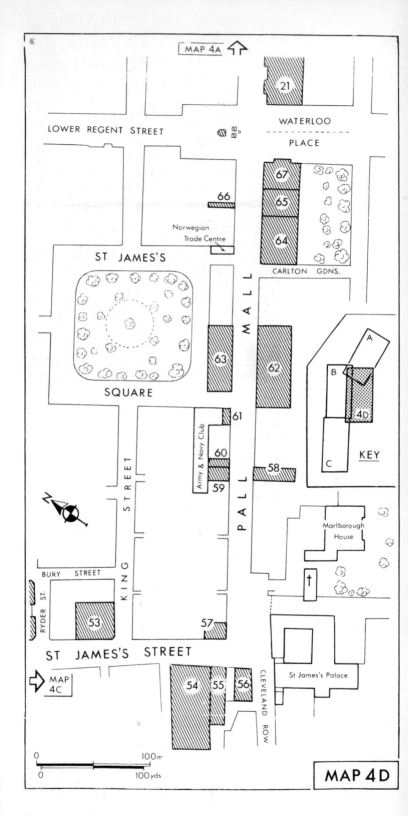

MAP 4A

21

WATERLOO

LOWER REGENT STREET

PLACE

67

65

66

64

Norwegian
Trade Centre

ST JAMES'S

CARLTON GDNS.

A

MALL

B

63

62

4D

SQUARE

KEY

C

Army & Navy Club

61

60

58

59

PALL

Marlborough
House

BURY STREET

KING

RYDER ST.

53

57

ST JAMES'S STREET

54  55  56

CLEVELAND ROW

MAP
4C

St James's Palace

0          100 m
0          100 yds

**MAP 4D**

*Rothmans, Pall Mall*
(**57**)

Shaw touches include the bold arches at ground floor level picked out in radial bands of stone alternating with brick and the use of decorated brick panels. There are sunflowers and foliage, as well as rows of garlanded cherubs, all fashioned in sculpted red brick—the symbols of the Aesthetic Movement of the 1880's and 1890's (Barnard, 1973).

There is very little to say about Pall Mall west end, except to note the constant use of white Portland Stone, and the constant threat of demolition and redevelopment (1982–83). Set within the limestone cliff stands **Schomberg House (58)**, strikingly different in its plum-red 17th century brickwork with white stone dressings. This was the large town-house of one of the Dutchmen brought to England by William of Orange, and survives rather remarkably in a street which has seen many changes both in character and in the building materials employed over the years. The eye-catching twisted caryatids which support the door porch, as well as the Wedgewood-like plaques high on the walls, are fashioned in Coade Stone, the most famous of the 17th–18th century artificial stone pastes later replaced

by fired Doulton ware.

On the north side of Pall Mall opposite, there are one or two modern buildings which at least break the Portland Stone stranglehold, one of which is the office of the **Phoenix Assurance Company (59)**, rebuilt in 1967 by Ronald Ward and Partners. There are several different stones involved here, the most prominent being the grey granite with the slight brown flecking, which is Creetown Granite from the Southern Uplands near Dalbeattie. It is used in the entrance pillars as well as in the foyer. The entrance step and flooring are of Italian Travertine, while the window surround has panels of 'Black Granite' of unknown source. The offices next door, **No. 43 Pall Mall (60)**, have an outer frame of dark grey foliated Rubislaw Granite with inside slabs of the other Aberdeenshire granite, Peterhead, as a colour contrast. The marble floor has inserts of Swedish Green Marble, again to add a colour contrast, while the side walls of the foyer are lined by sheets of pale veined brown marble which may be the French Breche Nouvelle. Completing this northern pavement, the **Bahamas High Commissioners Office (61)** is really but part of a larger unit which

95

is the Army & Navy Club with its main entrance in St James's Square. As a renewed building it was designed by T. P. Bennet in 1962, principally with cladding of Portland Stone (now rather smutty and besmirched) set off at ground level by rather opulent facings of 'Black Granite'. This particular variety is distinctive on account of its striking olive green mottling and flecks of bronzy pyrite. Best seen in the well-tended entrance to the Club off St James's Square, this may be the diorite from Herrestad near Jönköping in south-central Sweden.

Looking southwards once again we have to say about what is acknowledged to be an architecturally important building, the **Royal Automobile Club (62)**, that geologically it is no great monument— Portland Stone and rather dingy. As it was designed to a Parisian boulevard scale by Mewès & Davis (1908–11), it follows that the interior involves some rather splendid columns and panels of rich antique marbles, particularly those of Central Italy. Perhaps it would pay a dividend to join the R.A.C. to be able to go inside and study the marble at your leisure.

Directly opposite the R.A.C. used to be the **Junior Carlton Club** but all that was rebuilt in 1966 as an extremely long-fronted unit for Pall Mall, and equally unusual in that it has see-through glass and open-ness to the outside World. The new building, **30–35 Pall Mall (63)** has several geological features to note. First, at pavement level there are grey striped panels which appear to be slabs of Burlington Slate, a Silurian slabstone quarried in the south Lake District in what used to be part of Lancashire. As usual, these slabs have been cut with the cleavage and so show true bedding as a colour banding running across the surfaces. The same slate also comes into the building in thin horizontal courses along with Portland Roach, as contrast to the overall cladding of smooth Portland Whit-Bed.

We have now reached what is architecturally the most important sector of Pall Mall, buildings which were influential to design not just for London Clubs but for a whole range of commercial buildings which 'bor-rowed their clothes' as if to gain respectability (Summerson, 1976). Foremost amongst these is Barry's **Reform Club (64)** built in 1841 when he was already deeply involved in work for the Houses of Parliament. In strong contrast to the pointed Gothic of Westminster, he was able to work out an adaptation of the mediaeval classicism of Italy in a design which owes much to the Palazzo Farnese in Rome (Binney, 1969). Barry had earlier completed the **Travellers Club** next door **(65)** in an Italian Renaissance style, but comparatively delicate in details and built in brick and stucco. The **Reform Club** in contrast, faced with 'dirty Portland Stone', has visibly stronger pediments to the windows and a heavy cornice to the roofline, details which stand out the stronger when seen alongside the adjacent Travellers Club.

Opposite the Clubs, there are several points of interest on the north pavement. In the **Norwegian Trade Centre** there is sight of lustrous Otta Schist, a high grade metamorphic rock appropriately from the Caledonide mountains of Central Norway. A grander display comes in **No 14 Pall Mall (66)** where pillars, arches and columns are of polished giant feldspar Lamorna or Carnmenellis Granite from Cornwall. A true porphyry, the large orthoclase feldspar crystals show clear evidence of zoned growth through the concentrations of magnetite grains.

It is fitting to end this walk on the pavement outside the **Athenaeum. (67)** a building of 1828–30 which set the standard and style for the Clubs of St James's. Decimus Burton's Club is of very simple external line and is Bath Stone heavily disguised beneath gleaming white stucco. Inside, we are told, there are columns of brown artificial marble (Pevsner, 1962); outside, in elongate panels which form a low wall lending privacy to the basement windows, there is the genuine article in pieces of green Connemara Marble from the Dalradian of the west of Ireland. Here our walk stops, but geology goes on apparently endlessly through the streets of London, for as long and as far as you care to trace it.

*Boodles Club,*
*St James's Street,*
*overtopped by*
*The Economist*

*View along Pall Mall*
*West*

*Bloomsbury rooflines and Malet Street from University College*

# BLOOMSBURY AND ST. PANCRAS

For a Bloomsbury walk, there is a lot to be said for starting at the north front of The British Museum, close to the lions which guard the entrance. Behind us is The King Edward VIIth Gallery, a 20th century extension to the Museum which conforms to the pattern set for civic buildings of the Edwardian period—massive and imposing. To the left and right of us, we catch a glimpse of the trees which make the Bloomsbury squares so important a feature of the district generally, trees which were a part of the design of Burton and Cubitt when they laid out their terraces of town houses for the Bedford Estate. Such has been the piecemeal redevelopment of the area that the only sight we can get of such town houses from where we stand is the dark-weathered brickwork of the terraces which face on to Gower Street. To the north the sky is filled with the mass of Senate House, an academic ziggurat of 1932—a time when such buildings were of solid stone through and through, so that it contains enough Portland Stone to 'clad' at least three modern blocks of equal area.

Geologically the Bloomsbury heartland is monotonously uniform in either Portland Stone or stock brick with stucco renderings, so much so that paving stones, kerbs and cobbles may present the most intriguing challenge as we walk about. Ian Nairn summarised his own view of the architecture of the area thus: 'The splendid plane trees are still there to soothe when the strain of looking at the buildings becomes too great. But instead of gay but discreet stock brick surroundings, there are doughy intrusions like the droppings of an elephant' (Nairn, 1966). In our geological walk, we shall pick our way around the elephant droppings as best we can, slipping first westwards into the modern commercialism of Tottenham Court Road, for this is where there are richer veins to explore.

Starting with the **King Edward VIIth Gallery**, (**1**) however, this was designed by the Scot, Sir Thomas Burnet in 1904–1914 to match and extend the core of Smirke's British Museum of the mid-19th century. Compared with the classical lines of the old Museum, with its deep quadrangle space, backed by the broad flights of steps of Carboniferous sandstones from Bradford and Craigleith, the north face is flat and continuous. It lacks the projecting wings, and the pedimented entrance. If this sounds like an architectural criticism, it isn't; rather it is a geologists' disappointment that there is not more stonework to be seen here, and at closer quarters. As it is, what we can see is predominantly Portland Stone, rather yellowed with age, and interestingly

*Portland Stone Lions, British Museum (**1**)*

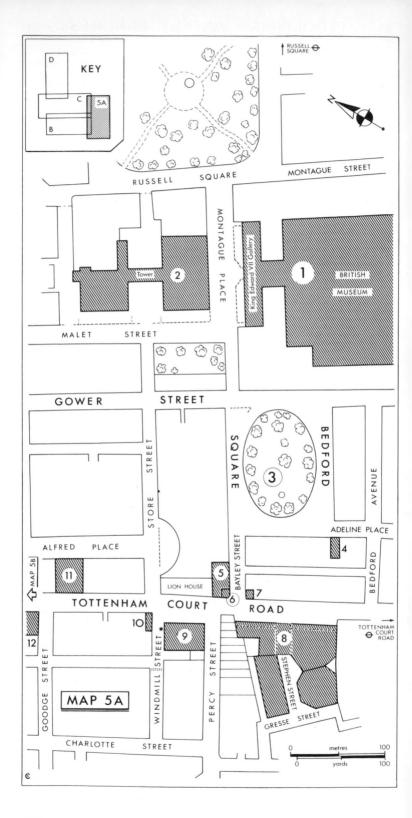

weathered so as to reveal the fossil content. Coupled with the limestone about the Egyptian-style entrances, and in the kerbing which once carried substantial railings, there are courses of dark grey granite—Carnsew Granite from quarries at Penryn to the north of Falmouth. Details are best seen in the smooth-rubbed surfaces of the wing entrances at both ends of the North Front, where a fabric can be made out within the granite in which dark mica flakes impart a close-felted texture, as well as a colour tone which is darker than for most Cornish granites. Quartz and orthoclase feldspar crystals occur as seed-like cores, white or pink against the grey groundmass of the rock. Finer in grain than other granites which we have seen, this may relate to the position of the Carnsew intrusion towards the outer margins of the larger Falmouth granite mass. Once again, the axe-dressed finish to the stone prevents the fullest appraisal of the actual texture and mineral composition of the rock—a sad limitation to the fullest appreciation of an igneous rock.

Turning now to the sedimentary rock of the North Front, the pillars, pedestals and copings of the railed area provide us with several different aspects of the Portland Stone when we look around. Starting with the lions for example, they have weathered to a whiteness which is almost chalky in appearance. Their line is visibly reduced to a rounded and softened outline as a result of steady loss of surface over the last 40 years. The same loss of surface in the upright pillars has thrown into relief, cross-bedding and bedding through the contrast between shell-rich and non-shelly limestone layers. In other parts there can be seen prominent oval patches which stand out from the surface. These are algal pellets—denser calcitic mud precipitated by the activities of lime-forming or lime-trapping algal sheets upon the tidal flats of the Upper Jurassic Portland Sea. Generally, the Portland Stone here shows less of the normal 'freestone' quality of the limestone and more of the bedded character of normal limestones.

Although it is some fifteen to twenty years younger than the Museum, the Portland Stone of **Senate House** (2) is notably whiter and as 'chalky' as the museum lions. There are exceptions to this condition. Some corners and less-exposed surfaces are dark-streaked and som-

*Senate House from Malet Street* (**2**)

bre, prompting ideas that exposure and local climate may have something to do with the whiteness of buildings, but altogether, this is a field in which facts are limited at present. At ground level, many of the blocks of limestone show large fossil fragments projecting to such an extent that it is possible to calculate that there must have been several millimetres loss of surface since the blocks were laid. At base, Senate House has the customary granite course, which is here up to half a metre in height. Once again, this stone is axe-dressed, but through its roughened surface, it appears very similar to the Cornish Carnsew Granite of The British Museum. Within the windswept ground-floor entrance foyer, the paving and the interior walls are of coarse-textured Italian travertine—a rock type which the Senate House architect, Charles Holden, used extensively in his other city buildings, notably in the Underground stations which he designed.

At this point, we do well to slip into the elegance of **Bedford Square** (**3**) via Montague Place and savour the balance and integrity of a piece of 18th century planning which survives and which has experienced a measure of renewal in recent years. The Square was laid out about the year 1775, still within the life-span of Capability Brown, and at the beginning of that of Humphrey Repton his son-in-law, who was to be responsible for Russell Square to the east. Here, there are terraces to north, south, east and west, facing in upon a railed central garden with mature London Plane trees. The terraces remain remarkably intact, with their grey brick set off by the arched doorways, prominently picked out in white-painted Coade Stone (heavily vermiculated). Each arch has a keystone decorated with a bearded head. These are minor details, however, to a grand design which sees each terrace with a central pedimented core, fully faced with white-painted stucco rendering. Admittedly this frame to the Square is almost non-geological, but part of the whole design remains the wide paving and the kerbing, which immediately become points to observe. Most of the paving slabs are of Carboniferous Coal Measure sandstones, probably from the West Riding of Yorkshire. They are finely laminated sandstone of a grey-green hue, which have become interesting from the foot-tread of years. Wear of the surface has broken through the top laminations to reveal lower layers which outcrop as concentric lines within the slabs. Some show an undulation which must represent a slight development of ripple-mark.

Turning to the kerbstones, most of the older ones are dark blue stone, probably diorite from the Channel Islands or dolerite from the Midlands, or dull red which is almost certainly the fine grained Mountsorrel Granite from Charnwood Forest. Of more recent times (1981), the dog's ear kerbs which narrow down the road skirting the central garden, are of a fine-grained silver-grey

*Bedford Square, north pavements (**3**)*

*Peterhead columns,
39 Bedford Square*
(**4**)

granite which is thought to be Bosahan Granite from quarries near Falmouth. The traffic flow in the Square is something of a hazard, so the kerbs are best studied from the safety of the pavement.

No such worry need concern you when taking in the splendid bulgy pillars of pink Peterhead Granite which support the porch entrance to **No. 39 Bedford Square** (**4**) in the southwest corner where it joins with Adeline Place. On the recently cleaned surfaces, you can see the limpid clear quartzes set within a framework of rather long feldspar laths which lend their colour to the rock as a whole. The steps and other stone dressings are of Portland Stone.

Leaving the Square by the northwest corner, Bayley Street, the upper levels of the **Bedford Corner Hotel** (**5**) deserve a glance. The walls are of grey brick with the complex arches of the windows picked out in yellow brick and Coade Stone mouldings. Flanking the windows are turned and polished columns of Peterhead Granite which, with the wrought iron balconies to each window, are details which may have been borrowed from the Grosvenor Hotel in Victoria—the archetype of late-Victorian–Edwardian hotels in London. Much more tangible geology comes in the large slabs of serpentinite which face **Barclays Bank** (**6**) in the ground floor space borrowed from the hotel at the corner to Tottenham Court Road. The surfaces are a deep mossy green colour, with fine fibrous veins ramifying through the rock to give a very convincing serpent-skin pattern to the slabs overall. This kind of serpentinite is cut from pod-like masses of reconstituted igneous rock (mainly basic or ultrabasic), found in the deeper root zones of mountain belts. In Europe, the Alps of Savoy or the Thessalonikan Mountains of northern Greece are the principal sources for this kind of stone which is so popular with stone-fitters.

Turning to the opposite side of the road (the south side), the black walls of **Swan Travel** (**7**) are lustrous slabs of almost jet-black larvikite in which the normally steel-blue feldspars have assumed a metallic bronze lustre. This rock is the recurring element in the extensive Tottenham Court Road frontage to this building, in spite of the multitude of individual shop fronts which slot in at pavement level. When we identify the main entrance (No. 247), we find wall surfaces of Italian Arebescato Marble, a finely veined white marble from the Carrara district of Apennine Italy. In contrast, the dark slabs which face the lifts at the back of the foyer are Devonian Torquay Marble. They are figured and patterned by pale patches which are colonies of *Stromatopora* and more straggling coral growths that made up reef masses in warm, subtropical seas in southwest England 340 million years ago.

Opposite, on the west side of Tottenham Court Road, there stands the new EMI complex, **Centre Cross** (**8**), a giant superstructure of decks underpinned by massive stilt legs which allow Stephen Street to tunnel through to Gresse Street on the other side. It is the supporting pillars to this road, and the arcading which fronts the shops, which provide us with excellent polished surfaces of Baltic Brown Granite, a very special variety of granite with prominent feldspar phenocrysts, coming from

*Centre Cross building, Tottenham Court Road (**8**)*

the shores of the Gulf of Finland close to the Russo–Finnish border. Baltic Brown is a typical rapakivi granite, a rock type extensive in the outcrops of the Precambrian of northern Scandinavia, but particularly in Finland and central Sweden. In Centre Cross, the brown rapakivi is offset by the pale orange Sardinian Beige Granite from the Sassari district in the northern part of the island. Unfortunately, this second granite is not easy to see at close quarters unless you go to the rear of the building in Stephen Street.

Moving north up Tottenham Court Road, we come to the corner of Percy Street and the limit of a surviving range of 18th century houses which in their time housed William Cowper, Wyndham Lewis, Vanessa Bell and Duncan Grant. What survives are several good door cases and windows, but all overshadowed by the towering mass of **Metropolis House** (**9**), set back from the line of the main thoroughfare by a wide strip of paving. From this viewpoint, we can take in the strange mixture of red brick and livid orange terracotta (in the attached pilasters and odd curly capitals) which make up **Lion House** (1905), a direct continuation from the Bedford

Corner Hotel, and a contemporary transition from residential to commercial utility.

Metropolis House affords one or two points of geology for our interest. Starting with the branch of the Midland Bank at its southwest corner, the facings to the building are ceramic tile cubes in bright red and white. Close to the night safe, and in the pillars which separate the bank from **Lasky's** next door, are surfaces of the rich red Swedish Imperial Granite. This is a fine-grained rock with a strong component of dark minerals, mainly biotite mica and ?hornblende, which with the red feldspars give a distinctive texture overall. A second geological detail to Metropolis House can be picked up when we stand back and look up at the tower which springs from the broad two-floor base. Then we see that there are slightly greyer horizontal bands crossing the cream coloured Portland Stone cladding of the greater part of the surface. The nature of the greyer rock is revealed in the lower walling to Windmill Street where, on both sides of the entrance to the underground car park (*), the grey rock turns out to be rough-riven cleavage slabs of Norwegian Otta Schist. The surfaces are

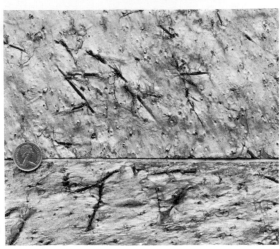

*Otta Schist Panels Lasky's*

roughened by crenulations, but also by the projection of match-stick-like crystals of hornblende up to 6 cm long, which have grown within the rock as it was metamorphosed. If you want to appreciate the characteristics of a high grade mica schist, this street outcrop is one of the places to visit.

At the corner of Windmill Street with Tottenham Court Road, stands **The Rising Sun** (10), a pub justly famous for its Art Nouveau elegance in stucco and terracotta decoration, but equally we might say, for its quota of natural stone. This comes in at pavement level where the strong verticals of the building are picked out in wedge-shaped pillars of rich dark larvikite, from which the feldspars shimmer with a silvery lustre from the intensely black base. The Rising Sun was designed by Treadwell & Martin in 1897 (find the date in the midst of the stucco-work) which then becomes an early date for the use of this well-known Norwegian syenite on London streets.

There is little further to note in walking up the road, but from the west side pavement, you can glance up and take in a range of very varied frontages, with odd touches of terracotta or rubbed brick, and more rarely, natural stone. Notice the broad panel across the front of **Paperchase** (11), which appears to be a vivid green example of Swedish (Green) Marble. This is a true marble quarried from the highly deformed and altered mountains of central Sweden, where impure limestones caught up in the folded succession of rocks, have had their clay minerals reformed and sometimes segregated to give the strong green chlorite or epidote streaks to the rock as a whole. In Britain, marbles from the Precambrian of Connemara and Iona are very similar to this Swedish marble, but are now much less readily available as building stone.

Where Goodge Street joins Tottenham Court Road, stands what used to be **Catesby's**, a furnishing store of old-world character and of a status just a little less than Maples. Catesby's passed away in the late 1950's, but their old building remains as a piled up fantasy, which needs to be appreciated from the distance of Alfred Place to capture the full effect (**12**). From there, the eye can run up the height of the building to its neatly slated turrets and pinnacles of a restless roof-line. En routè, your gaze could take in bulging bow-windows, heavy balconies and much decoration, all in Portland Stone. What catches the eye most, however, must be the bold arches at ground floor level, framed in a plum red rock which is mainly Swedish Virgo Granite, once combined with one or two columns of Shap Granite. In 1980, there was a fire in the ground floor area which burned so fiercely that some of the granite surround was cracked and flaked to such an extent that much of the stonework had to be renewed. The match is not too good, as a Virgo-type granite with the distinctive blue or violet coloured quartz crystals is not easily available nowadays. If you study the columns to No. 67, you can judge the outcome of the repair.

A Golden Egg restaurant used to

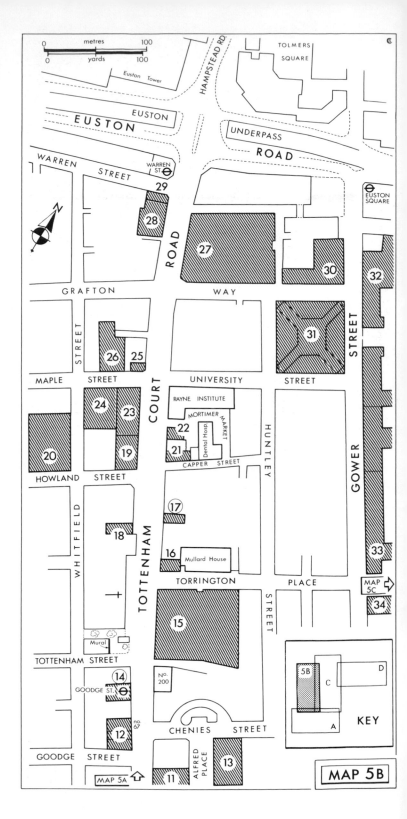

MAP 5B

*Ex-Catesby building, Goodge Street, now Guggenheims*

occupy the Goodge Street corner of the Catesby Building, employing a striking and instructive Devonian Red Belgian marble in its frontage. In 1984 this gave way, alas, to the chromium and glass of Guggenheims. *Sic transit gloria. . . .*

It is now worthwhile turning briefly into Alfred Place to take in the large black tower of **Whittington House** (**13**). This is really a building to see in afternoon sun, when it reflects the light in a striking mirror fashion for a building of dark overall colour. Built in 1970–72 to the design of Richard Seifert, black Rustenberg Gabbro from the Bushveld Complex south of Pretoria was the facing stone chosen and fitted with near-invisible joins to these sheer wall faces, broken only by the stainless steel window frames of unusual Moorish shape. If Metropolis House is our standard for

metamorphic schist, then Whittington House could serve equally for 'Black Granite', or more correctly, gabbro. Inside, other natural stones figure in the ground floor foyer, including Sicilian Pearl Marble in the flooring, and the fawn-grey French Breche Nouvelle Marble on the facing walls. These are matters of legitimate interest to us, but be warned, Whittington House is now Government premises where security precautions make it embarrassing to follow up geological curiosity too far.

Back in Tottenham Court Road, look across to the full height of **Goodge Street Underground Station** (**14**), topping one of the deepest lift shafts to the whole underground system. Up to and including the second floor, the station is faced in the highly-glazed plum-coloured

*Tottenham Court Road, looking north*

Doulton tile which is almost the trade mark of the Bakerloo and Northern lines of the turn of the century. Proof against pollution of all kinds, it added a touch of colour to the streets as well as self-advertisement for the service. Colour of a more recent kind comes close-by in the contemporary mural which decorates the gable-end of a shop in Tottenham Street and faces on to the open space of the old burial ground of Whitfield's Chapel—a welcome resting place from the traffic and crush of pedestrians on Tottenham Court Road. From this sanctuary, you can take in the relatively clean and simple lines of **Heal's**, built in 1916 to the design of Smith & Beaver (**15**). The steel-framed building is clad in Portland Stone in a way which seems to convey that internal framework through stone verticals and horizontals which are anything but massive and ponderous (as they can be in other buildings of that period, No. 200 to the south for example).

During 1984, Heal's underwent an extensive refit as it merged with Habitat, producing interesting exposures at street level which deserve attention. While the main facing to the older building on Tottenham Court Road is Portland Stone, the substantial pillars to the pavement are of the slightly cream-coloured Hopton Wood Stone from north of Wirksworth in Derbyshire. This is a limestone composed of small broken shell fragments set in a fine lime groundmass. It has two outstanding characteristics. Firstly, it has 'free-stone' quality, being capable of dressing in all directions with equal ease. Secondly, it is a stone which has 'marble' quality in that it can be rubbed smooth and takes and retains a polish. As such, it is a natural stone which has been sought by sculptors and monumental masons as one of our best native stones. Geologically, its Carboniferous age is evident from the small crinoid ossicles (perforated discs of calcite) which can be detected on the polished surfaces. To match it in the newer work, the northern extension to Heal's on Torrington Street sees the same robust pillars faced in a corn-brown Jurassic limestone (thought to be French) crowded with shell fragments including a few identifiable bivalves and showing occasional burrows as either darker or lighter patches against the general background. The best surfaces, because they are more uniformly polished, are to be

*Mullard House,*
*Torrington Street*
**(16)**

found close to the main entrance, where the hallway is lined with highly polished Italian Travertine (of late Tertiary age, and from Tivoli, near Rome). Another geological touch in the original Heal's is the small inlay tablets of green Connemara Marble, seen in the heavy glass skylights set in the pavements along the frontage of the 1916 core to the premises.

War-time bomb damage and rebuilding mean that all the territory north of Heal's is of the 1950's or 60's, with only one or two late additions of the more recent past. This makes this stretch of Tottenham Court Road very different from what has gone before and, as is typical for the period, the natural stone attached to fairly standard office blocks can vary widely in both type and provenance. This is the case with **Barclays Bank** on the corner with Torrington Street **(16)**, which is really an extension of **Mullard House**. What we see most strikingly in both are large-area panels of rich, lustrous green serpentinite, the dark green tone lightened by the network of pale netveins. Periodic resurfacing to maintain the lustrous finish is very neces-

sary with this stone and has been the practice in this building over recent years. What has not been possible, however, is the maintenance of the exact colour of the original sepentinite through periods of replacement or reconstruction, as for example in the surround to the new cash dispenser. The newer stone has quite a different colour cast. The upper floors of the same buildings are faced with some rather suspect Portland Stone (cracked and stained in appearance), offset by thin vertical strips of pale green Lake District Slate.

On the same side of the street, the next building to note is **The Iraqi Centre (17)**, whose deep arched frontage is framed by uprights of silver-grey Sardinian Granite (Sardinian Grey). In many respects, particularly texturally, this rock is similar to the Sardinian Beige Granite as seen in Centre Cross (see **8** above), except for the body colour of the orthoclase feldspar. The pale granite here is set off by the use of intensely black Ebony Black gabbro in the bases to the windows.

On the west side of Tottenham Court Road, **Lloyds Bank (18)** has one special geological offering in the

*Iraqi Centre, Tottenham Court Road (**18**)*

shape of panels of vividly bright Swedish Green Marble above and around the night safe. The marble is banded by brown veins which seem to parallel the foliation direction, but which are pinched-out at intervals in a manner which suggests further stress following the original deformation. The colour of this Swedish marble is a deeper copper-green than the softer yellow-green of most Connemara Marble (as seen in the pavement skylights outside Heal's down the road). Apart from this touch of marble, the bank and the rest of this west side block involves large polished panels of larvikite at pavement level, with Portland Stone upper walling. In the entrance to the apartments within the same block there is a buff coloured stone which could easily be mistaken for off-white Portland Stone. Closer scrutiny will show that this is a richly bioclastic limestone with an 'oatmeal' texture, which is Nabresina Marble from the Cretaceous close to Trieste in the northern Adriatic. Sometimes called Roman Stone, this is a beautifully even-grained limestone, quite unaltered by processes which would be involved in the formation of a true marble.

Continuing on the west side of the road, across Howland Street, the **National Westminster Bank (19)** has large panels of dense Ebony Black 'black granite', in which the outline of what must originally have been feldspar crystals can be picked out in oblique lighting by filigree patterns of metallic replacement and

intrusion. Highly altered like most 'black granites', there is no easy way of telling the original character of the rock (?granite, ?gabbro or ?syenite) other than to recognise that in this case it was coarse-grained and poor in quartz. No such problems arise with the slabs of the front steps, which are either Cornish Cheeswring or De Lank Granite from Bodmin Moor—a grey-brown groundmass granite, with elongate phenocrysts of orthoclase feldspar of medium size (see Dangerfield & Hawkes, 1981).

Next door, the deep-set entrance to No. 97, the **Department of Employment (20)** has walling lined with a rusty-mottled travertine, interesting for the tubules which crowd across obvious bedding planes. These tubules must have been crusts which formed about the roots and stems of aquatic plants which grew in ancient spring deposits. Elsewhere, there are small gastropods concentrated in lenses within this rock, all of which adds to the environmental picture we can build up for the conditions of its formation—a Tertiary petrifying spring.

At this point, it is as well to look across the road to take in the buildings of the east side. To the right, at the corner with Capper Street, **The Mortimer Arms (21)** is faced with the micaceous cleavage splits of Italian Barge Quartzite, a high-grade metamorphic granulite from the mountains of Savoy. As seen here and in other Truman houses (for which this is a kind of trade-mark), Barge Quartzite is grey or buff, the colours mixed to give an overall mottling to the building. Extremely hard wearing and proof against all pollutants other than aerosol sprays, Barge Quartzite is a very serviceable building material for cities and an alternative to the universal Portland Stone. In **No. 170** Tottenham Court Road, the metamorphic rock is set alongside the fiercely red brick and brown glass of the complex designed by Llewellyn–Davies and Partners to house the **Rayne Institute (22)** and the Dental Hospital of University College, extending from Capper Street to University Street. At pavement level, the shop units set into this complex, offer extensive surfaces of an attractive igneous rock which is Dakota Mahogany Granite. Study of the polished surfaces will show that this rock has large pink crystals of orthoclase feldspar (rather square and stumpy) as well as more slender plagioclases (lath-shaped). The dark patches are either green hornblende or a biotite mica. Quartz is present as lucid grey patches within the brown groundmass. Some of the slabs are crossed by thin feldspathic veins, indicating that this American rock has much in common with older Caledonide granites of the Scottish Highlands. Dakota Mahogany comes from the Precambrian Shield of North America as it emerges from beneath the Prairies to form the Black Hills of Dakota. It seems to have become popular with architects

in the 1970's, possibly on account of its warm brown colour. Its greatest exposure in London is probably in the Angel Court development off Lothbury at the very heart of the City.

The **National Westminster Bank** on the opposite side of the road (**23**) is technically part of the Portland Stone-clad Matthew Hall House, a frame unit building of a type generally common in this area between Charlotte Street and Tottenham Court Road. In the case of the bank, the pavement course is some 1.5 m of grey Barge Quartzite, passing up into polished window sills of ?Penryn Granite. The dark upright pillars prove to be of Carboniferous Limestone through the occurrence of very small crinoid ossicles within the dark groundmass of the stone.

**Matthew Hall House** itself (**24**) has several additional rock types. The same black Carboniferous Limestone appears as the massive round pillars of the entrance (the fitting of the curved segments to form the drum sections is a skill worth noting), the crinoid ossicles being accompanied by diagnostic cross-sections of the small coral *Zaphrentites* on the north face of the column closest to the door. The provenance of the limestone is uncertain, but dark limestones of this type often come from quarries close to Tournai in Belgium. Alternatively, the stone could have come from quarries in southern Ireland. The foyer to the building is lined by panels of the grey and white marble

*Matthew Hall House, Tottenham Court Road* (**24**)

Grigio Fiorito Timau from the Devonian of northern Italy, the pattern of veining having been carefully matched up to create a kaleidoscopic image in this highly polished stone. This same true marble is to be found in the external walling to Maple Street, where its' pock-marked and weathered surfaces demonstrate that such polished marbles are not the material for out of doors in the British climate.

Across Maple Street in the front of **The Roebuck** (**25**) there is affirmation that nothing really can compare with good quality, well-finished igneous rock, demonstrated by the dark toned larvikite, matched with the deep red Swedish Balmoral Granite. Next door to the Roebuck on Maple Street is a building. **British Telecom** (**26**), where the vertical pillars which face the street and divide the windows show another limestone of marble quality, at present with a polished finish. The rock is Napoleon Tigre, a Carboniferous Limestone from the Pas de Calais. It was popular in Edwardian times for its warm buff colour and the 'figuring' of the slabs, which stems from

the sedimentary structures which are found in shallow-water, algal limestone muds as they dry out. Clear calcite infills the desiccation cracks and gives a tiger-striping to the rock as a whole.

Walking northwards again, the next milestone must be the new-style **Maples** which was unveiled in 1979 (**27**). The original store had a very distinctive character as a building as much as an established British institution in the world of home furnishing. So much so, that its white-icing exterior with its end towers, resembling those of Wembley Stadium, would have been scheduled for conservation as a matter of course if redevelopment had been delayed until the more sensitive 1980's. As it is, what emerged from the complete renewal of the site was the introduction of large surface areas of the grey-brown Rivière à Pierre Granite from southern Quebec province, close to the United States border. Granites of this type are one of the major exports of Quebec. They are generally of the same age as those of the Scottish Highlands or the Lake District. Good

*Maples, corner of Grafton Way (**27**)*

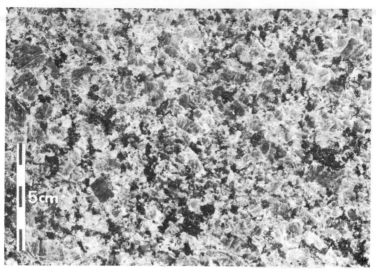

*Detail of Canadian Granite, Grafton Way (27)*

surfaces for study can be found at the northern end to Maples (the offices of ITV), or in the better exposed (to sunlight) surfaces on Grafton Way to the south side of the block.

The western side of Tottenham Court Road seldom gets bright sunlight, but the newly cleaned frontage to the **Grafton Hotel (28)** shows the distinctive orange brown tone of Bath Stone. Much more recent in date is **McDonalds (29)** opposite the Tube Station, which sports in its frontage the rock types which have become as much their advertising symbol as the uniforms of their staff. These rock types are polished travertine combined with touches of black Rustenberg Bon Accord Gabbro. The travertine is a rather solid variant to the range of rocks which are bracketed under this one name. The striking feature of this variant is the strong colour contrast between white limestone bands and layers of green mud. It is possible that the white bands are of algal origin, fractured by shrinkage and rupture soon after formation. Nowadays there is a wide range of different travertines, some with strong colour and textural contrasts, being used by the stone-fitting trade. Much of the range still comes from Italy, but now we could add almost any southern European country as a possible source, provided there are Tertiary or sub-Recent tuffaceous spring deposits in their stratigraphical column. Whatever their source, it remains true that the modes of origin of travertines and their textural variations are a study still to receive proper attention from geologists. For our part, it is sufficient that the slumping, incipient folding and faulting of the strongly colour-contrasted St. John's Travertine of McDonalds could occupy our attention for quite some time, to the curiosity of the patrons inside.

Getting back to our progress through Bloomsbury, we now move to Gower Street by way of Grafton Way, so coming upon the two separate buildings which make up **University College Hospital**. We might start by looking at the newer of the two, the Accident and Outpatients Wing on the north side of the street **(30)**. This is a frame building of the late 1950's, with cladding of Portland Stone (rather dirty and smeared by downwash of lime) and horizontal panels of Dolerite Stone Aggregate (large chips of crushed dolerite, bedded in cement panels). At pavement level and about the entrance, however, there are some very good facing slabs of Lake District Green Slate, which, as has been explained earlier, is a form of volcanic ash ejected from a volcanic vent, transported and redeposited by flowing water, then finally toughened up by deforming pressures which were responsible for the 'slate' character of the final rock. The main interest in the panels in Grafton Way lies in the fact that they display coarser-grained ash eroding channels into finer-grained material, filling the scooped-out hollows with current-bedded layers.

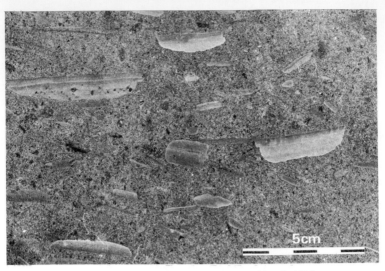

*Lake District Slate, University College Hospital* (**31**)

From time to time, there is evidence that there was slumping of the wet sands. Just to the right of the main entrance, one panel shows no fewer than three erosional channels in close association. As is often the case, the slabs are mounted so that the original bedding direction is quite strongly swung out of line.

Nothing could be a stronger contrast to what we have just been looking at than the older Hospital on the other side of the street. **University College Hospital,** of an older generation, was built to an overall design by Alfred Waterhouse between 1897 and 1906, employing his favourite materials, hard red brick and fiery red terracotta, for the details and mouldings which included an enormous coat of arms high up on the north-facing wall (**31**). The hospital was built to its cruciform ground plan with the express design to bring the maximum amount of sunlight to the elongate wings throughout daylight hours. Fiery red, pinnacled and towered, it is not difficult to imagine the impact which this building must have had upon the sedate and uniform terrace fronts to Gower Street in the 1900's, although that might simply echo an earlier outcry when the new University of London (now University College London) thrust its way into the Bloomsbury squares a century earlier (1827).

At the time of its foundation, **University College** must have been something of a social and architectural shock to this hitherto undeveloped farmland on the outer fringe of the Bedford Estate, even though its arrival had been carefully planned to be acceptable aesthetically. The buildings had been designed by Wilkins on very classical lines, involving a tall columnate portico rising from a broad flight of steps leading from an open quadrangle, the whole being capped by a well-proportioned dome (**32**). For various reasons, the original plan to complete the quadrangle with a wing shutting off College from Gower Street was never completed, giving passing traffic a striking view of the dome and portico which promised to be there for all time. Now, however, the almost-scheduled view has been narrowed down to a fleeting glimpse as a result of the construction of end pieces to the previously incomplete wings (1983–84).

University College as built by Wilkins was classical in another sense in that the base course to the portico and wings is of axe-dressed Cornish Granite, topped by walls and columns of solid Portland Stone which form a kind of monument in themselves to the quality and character of that stone. The drum sections to the columns for example reach up to 1.5 m in height before you can detect a join, preceded usually by a band of shelly limestone. This unit of thickness coincides closely with the maximum bed-unit obtainable from either the Base Bed or Whit Bed of the Portland quarries, allowing a little trimming of waste from the top and bottom of the natural stratum. The horizontal attitude of the shell bands

*New entrance to University College London, April 1985* (**32**)

in the columns make it clear that the drums were cut with the bedding and set into the building with that same orientation. The expanded bases to the same columns have caught the rainwash and drips of over one hundred and fifty years, consequently, the once-sharp collar has become a pock-marked gutter. All the exposed surfaces of the stone appear to be whiter than the less-well exposed areas of column or wall, as is a 'splash zone' just above ground level, prompting the thought that exposure and local climate may have much to do with the surface hue of Portland Stone in buildings. A more direct cause-and-effect aspect lies in the badly worn treads to the steps. This has lead to some rather piecemeal repair work over the years. To complete the catalogue of problems associated with stone in City atmosphere, we could study the surfaces which face the podium at the foot of the stairs, on either side of the College War Memorial. We will see that the surfaces are crazed with a crust which spreads like lichen across the entire surface. Quite resistant to weak acid, it seems that this crust is a sulphate deposit, developed after long years of exposure of the pure limestone to a polluted atmosphere, including sulphur dioxide. The best stone is clearly that to be seen in the portico; the later wings on either side have not quite such good and lasting stone and show areas of water damage arising from overspill from

roof guttering, as well as extensive areas of pock-marked surface following dry sandblast cleaning treatment in 1980.

Leaving the quadrangle area, and moving down Gower Street, we come to the **Darwin Building** on Gower Street, and the **Engineering Building** facing on to Torrington Place (**33**) which represents College expansion in the 1960's at the expense of the pre-existing 'gloomy terraces of Gower Street' (*The Builder*, 1897). Both of these newer buildings are faced with very white Portland Stone which is already giving up its fossil content through a loss of surface of up to 5 mm over twenty years. Run your hand over the surfaces of the balustrade to test the veracity of this. What is equally evident are the patches of shell and algal limestone which pepper newer Portland Stone and also the problem presented by lime-downwash over sheer and continuous wall surfaces (notice the smears upon Darwin's blue plaque).

Round into Torrington Place, **Dillon's University Bookshop** (**34**) deserves a glance, directed especially to the first and second floors to take in the pinnacles, canopies and niches for non-existent statues, all fashioned in pinkish coloured terracotta—probably the product of the Doulton Works in Lambeth (1908–09). If you can decipher the scrolls in the decoration the motto '*Que Sera Sera*' should remind you that we are on the borders of the Bedford Estate

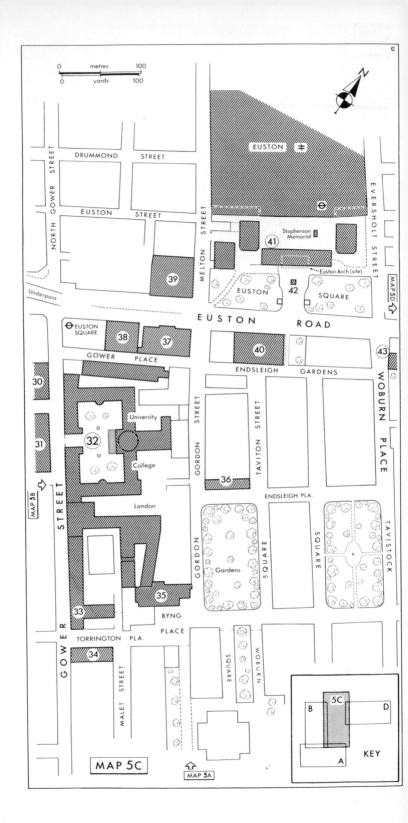

metres 100

yards 100

DRUMMOND STREET

EUSTON STREET

NORTH GOWER STREET

Underpass

EUSTON

MELTON STREET

EVERSHOLT STREET

Stephenson Memorial

41

Euston Arch (site)

EUSTON 42 SQUARE

E U S T O N R O A D

EUSTON SQUARE

38 37

GOWER PLACE

30

31

MAP 5B

University

32

College

London

STREET

GOWER

33

34

MALET STREET

TORRINGTON PLA.

39

40

ENDSLEIGH GARDENS

43

WOBURN PLACE

GORDON STREET

TAVITON STREET

36

ENDSLEIGH PLA.

GORDON SQUARE

Gardens

SQUARE

TAVISTOCK

35

BYNG PLACE

WOBURN SQUARE

MAP 5C

MAP 5A

MAP 5D

B 5C D

A KEY

116

*Dillon's University Bookshop, Torrington Place (34)*

and that the well laid-out squares and terraces which we approach, were the work of Thomas Cubitt and his sons as they converted the green-field sites into what is recognised as the essence of Bloomsbury, its town-house squares (Hobhouse, 1971). The whole area was set out as a speculative venture, hoping to attract the new middle class who worked in the growing commercial world of the City. Building went hand in hand with the improvement of the highways—the New Road connecting Marylebone with Islington—as well as with the development of the new railway terminals of Euston, Kings Cross, and later, St Pancras. Geological interest rests largely with the time of the development, when several important finds were made in the terrace sands and gravels of Endsleigh Place recording the animal life of one of the warm periods within the long time span of the Ice Age. Quite a different inheritance are the kerbstones and paving slabs, some of which survive from the initial planning of the area. For the most part, the terraces themselves are weak in natural stone, being brick disguised behind stucco facings with whatever there is in the way of ornament being fashioned in terracotta. Fortunately, there are exceptions to this general rule, some of them quite remarkable.

In Byng Place, for example, we come upon the considerable mass of the **Church of Christ the King (35)** at the southwest corner of Gordon Square. The church was built between 1851 and 1853 by the architect Brandon for the Catholic Apostolic Church, a thriving if exclusive sect with apocalyptic visions which cannot have included the thought that the church would never be completed, nor that it would have foundation problems. Designed to a cathedral scale, it should have had a central tower crowned by a high-proportioned steeple, as well as several additional bays to the nave. As it is, completed up to a cost of some £53,000, it ended up a considerable load and deadweight upon previously unconsolidated brickearth and terrace gravels, so much so that it caused the immediate collapse of a house in nearby Byng Place. This is a matter of interest to us today, for in spite of formidable brick under-vaulting which we can see from the pavement, the church itself shows certain signs of subsidence in the manner in which blocks have parted and joints opened up in the south wall. Other than this, our interest lies in the fact that the church was built of Bath Stone, recognisable for its orange-brown colour, as well as the tendency to weather almost black in less exposed quarters of the building. A further detail, best seen on the internal walls, is a pattern of veining which Arkell has referred to as 'watermark'—fine, slightly sinuous calcite veins, standing out as dark lines against the even tone of the stone. A less welcome trade mark of Bath Stone in London is its habit of blistering in damp sunless corners—a feature also to be seen here.

If we look at the walling to the

117

*The Church of Christ the King, Byng Place (35)*

pavements, and the gateway entrance from Byng Place, we can distinguish a second variety of Bath Stone which is a cross-bedded shelly limestone of the type which would be referred to as 'ragstone'. If these surfaces are studied with a hand lens, the rock will immediately be seen to be made up of layer upon layer of even-grained pellets (ooliths), separated by lines of accumulated shell fragments which have been selectively picked out by local wind erosion as projections. Locally, badly weathered stone has been cut out and replaced by new blocks, but more often by patches of reconstituted stone dust in a series of what might be called 'dentistry repairs'. While this may be structurally sound, and saving, as much can not be said for the visual effect, which strikes the eye quite blatantly as we scan the walls and move round into Gordon Square. The interior of the church is most impressive—an airy, cool cave in Bloomsbury in summer.

At the northern end of this garden square, stands the **Institute of Archaeology** of the University (**36**), a modern building which once again introduces to us Lake District Green Slate as a facing stone to the ground floor, the upper floors being of Portland Stone. As was the case with the newer part of the hospital (see **30** above), it is fascinating to trace the sedimentary structures preserved in this altered volcanic ash, although this is not so easy here on account of the rough-riven finish to the slabs. Nevertheless, broad colour contrasts run across these surfaces and allow us to pick out graded bedding from coarse layers to very fine, as well as the inclusion of larger fragments within the finer matrix. The proportion of such fragments, and the apparent poor sorting of some of the layers, give an impression of either periodic torrential flow of water, or else the raining down of air-borne clasts into the sediment as it accumulated. Either history could be true for the Borrowdale Volcanic Series of the central Lake District as read from the natural crag exposures of Langdale, Scafell or Honister.

Walking on northwards towards Euston on the west side of Gordon Street, you can still tread upon paving stones which are genuine Coal Measure flags from the West Riding of Yorkshire, or in the case of some of the greener coloured slabs, may be from the Caithness Flags of the far north of Scotland. This paving continues right up to Gower Place, when more and more of the slabs are of composite nature—rock chips in a cement matrix.

At this point we come up against the solid Portland Stone mass of the **Wellcome Institute** (**37**), a very solid building dating from 1931, when you can easily believe that the walling is of solid limestone blocks, through and through. Once again, it is useful to know the precise date of the building if only to assess the extent of the weathering in terms of sur-

*The Wellcome Institute, Euston Road* (**37**)

face-loss over the years. Such loss has probably been greatest from the low walling and coping slabs, where the usual large fragments of Jurassic oyster shell now stand clear from the worn-back surface of the lime-stone matrix. The main walling, re-cently cleaned most effectively by fine water spray techniques (1983), seems by comparison to have been less affected by erosion and weath-ering.

We have now reached Euston Road, but it is worth our while taking a short walk along Gower Place in order to take in the sunlit surfaces of the new **Unity House**, the headquar-ters building of the National Union of Railwaymen, which runs through from the Euston Road (**38**). The old Unity House was always a place of pilgrimage for geologists in that it was of solid Merrivale Granite from Dartmoor from ground to first floor levels (Elsden, 1923). The new build-ing is all clad in red-brown Dakota Mahogany Granite, a Mid-West intru-sive which we have seen earlier in Tottenham Court Road (see **22** above). Geologically the veined slabs and highly polished surfaces (espe-cially those to be seen in Gower Place) are a bonus to be appreciated, giving a clear understanding that this

American granite has undergone a measure of metamorphism which has imparted a gneissic character to the rock overall. Notice also the bluish colour cast of the quartz crystals as a sign of slight crushing.

If we now return to the junction of Gordon Street with the Euston Road, we can look around and take in the changing styles of the years. The Euston Road itself is a widened version of the 'The New Road', an improved turnpike road set up by Act of Parliament in 1756 to connect Paddington with Islington. Con-tinuously through the 19th century the road was widened, with first the gardens and then the terraced houses themselves being cleared on both sides. Even so, the line of the present road is quite erratic, particu-larly on the south side as we trace it to St Pancras.

On the north side, on the corner of Euston Square, stands the building designed by Beresford Pite for the **London, Edinburgh & Glasgow Insurance Company** in 1907 (**39**), involving Portland Stone as the prin-cipal material. In the Egyptian-style entrance there are columns of a strongly porphyritic Cornish Granite comparable with the variety Con-stantine from Carnmenellis. This gra-

*The L. E. & G. Insurance, Euston Road (**39**)*

nite has large, elongate orthoclase feldspar laths set against a very brown medium-grained groundmass, peppered with dark grains of magnetite and wisps of mica. Seen from a distance, the building is strange in having the appearance of having been finished and then extended by another floor in what looks like a completely different style (?Egyptian sitting on top of Greek), the whole then topped by three low-angled gables. Much more conventional is **Friends House** facing it across the junction (**40**), a building of 1927 in warm red brick, with dressings of Portland Stone, including the large columns to the Euston Road portico.

If we now turn to look north across the road to the restored Euston Square Gardens, we look at what to some is a battlefield of a defeat as poignant as Culloden to a Highlander. In 1960 there stood on the same ground an hotel, a cluster of indifferent buildings alongside it and, in the midst, Phillip Hardwick's Euston Arch—a triumphal arch copied from the Propylea to the Acropolis. In 1841, this same arch had been the triumphal and imposing entrance to the terminus of Robert Stephenson's London & Birmingham Railway—a truly impressive gateway to the Midlands and beyond. At that time, it had cost no less than £35,000, which could either be considered a bold and extravagant gesture or a striving after the 'Necessary Monument' (Crosby, 1970). By 1960 such valuations had declined and it was judged that there was no useful role for the Arch in the plan for a new Euston devised by British Rail. Protest was wide ranging and from a diversity of interests and in some ways it gave a purpose to The

Victorian Society, but in spite of all, demolition took place in 1961. Recriminations continue to this day, especially when it is appreciated that plans could have been adjusted to incorporate the same Arch into the present design (Smithson & Smithson, 1968).

What we lost, apart from a monument to the Industrial Revolution in Britain, was a considerable exposure of Bramley Falls Sandstone, hewn from quarries in the Millstone Grit north of Leeds, although the same stone survives in the massive walling to the cuttings of Euston Bank and in the tunnels beneath Primrose Hill. In place of all this, we have to admit that what replaced the Arch in the 'New Euston' is something of a geological bonus, for which we must be grateful. From a distance, the complex of towers and their substructure, stand out for their combination of shining black stone, stainless steel and glass. At close quarters, the black stone has the distinctive mottled texture which we have already seen in igneous rocks of the gabbro clan. The stone is Rustenberg Bon Accord Gabbro, already seen in Whittington House (stop **13** above), but here available in several slightly differing variants. Rustenberg Gabbro actually comes from some of the lower layers of the pile which makes up the Bushveld saucer-shaped intrusive complex, a level at which there are recognisable concentrations of chromite and other metallic ores within the fabric of the gabbro. In the Euston polished surfaces, we can detect these ores as metallic screens picking out for us the outlines of the original feldspar laths. Not all the panels are of the same texture or colour, some of

120

*British Rail House, from Friends House* (**41**)

them demonstrating coarser veining of lighter-coloured minerals; some of them showing crystal-filled inclusions. Clearly at Euston we have the maximum accessible exposure of South African Bushveld rocks available to the London geologist, either in the walling to **British Rail House** (**41**) or any of the nearby towers occupied by Fluor Ltd. All the buildings are internally fitted with walling and flooring faced with the buff coloured Italian Perlato Marble, a limestone crowded with brown shell fragments, and crossed by irregular coursed pressure-solution veins lined with brown clay. If you study any of these surfaces, you will quickly pick out bushy colonies of bryozoans, more compact colonies of calcareous algae, and a limited number of patterned cross-sections of hexacorals. Most interesting, however, must be the occasional clusters of thick-shelled bivalves (rudistids), which prove the warm-water, low-latitude origin for this particular limestone, and its Cretaceous age.

As we walk the wide spaces between the towers to reach the station proper, we cross surfaces of hard wearing industrial bricks which are Brown Brindles, made from the Coal Measure clays from the succession around Cannock Chase in Staffordshire—the source of much industrial earthenware and load-bearing brick. Out of this broad concourse there rises one survivor from the Euston Station of past years—the statue of Robert Stephenson which once stood in the famous Main Hall of the old terminus. He stands on a plinth of pink Peterhead Granite, which characteristically shows one or two small dark inclusions of schisty country rock within the even-texture of this familiar granite.

Passing on to the glass-fronted area of the booking hall and platforms we come to black vertical pillars which at first glance could be taken for plastic. Looked at more closely, and in low incident light, it is possible to pick out faint hieroglyphic patterns in bronze-lustred pyrite, which once again define for us an original texture of feldspar laths, and the appreciation that this is indeed a natural stone and another of the 'black granite' suite of rocks. The source for this particular rock is unknown, but it could well be one of the highly altered intrusives of southern India, Morocco or South Africa. One other test; if you tap the

*Kiosk to Euston Road*

seemingly solid pillar, it will give a hollow ringing tone, proving that the stone is only thin cladding sheets to the structural steelwork.

Moving back to the Euston Road, we pass the **L.N.W.R. War Memorial** to those who fell in the First World War (**42**), a monument which offers surfaces of Cornish Granite, possibly Cheeswring Granite from Bodmin Moor, but certainly one of those southwestern England granites in which the feldspar laths are prominent against a grey-brown groundmass, and equally clearly, show an alignment of the laths as either a record of fluid movement or growth under stress. The plinth itself is of very white Portland Stone, displaying a wide range of sedimentary structures, principally bedding and cross-bedding picked out as the shell-rich limestone has been etched by differential weathering. The same rock is to be seen in the two small lodges which flank the station approach from the Euston Road, their stonework scrubbed clean and slightly pock-marked following recent cleaning operations. They survive from the old Euston, in which they served as a 'front' to the outside world for an aggressive railway company—the L.N.W.R., which

set out to claim the custom of would-be-travellers who might be passing, unaware that they could travel to almost any destination from this very station. Swansea?, Dublin?, Tenby?—all were claimed for the L.N.W.R. according to the gilded names graven on to the tablets of the rusticated corner blocks of these lodges.

If we now cross the busy road, and slip through the quiet garden of Friends House, we can pass into **Endsleigh Gardens** for a good reason which is as much a matter of townscape as geology, for this is the best viewpoint from which to take in the elegance of the 'new' **St Pancras Parish Church** (**43**), with its prominent west tower and steeple crowning a classical pedimented portico. The church was built in 1822 by the Inwoods, father and son, to accommodate the needs of the growing population of the parish as the area grew in relation to the New Road on the one hand, and the terraced squares on the other.

The church predates the great debate as to what was the style which best befitted Christian places of worship, and so borrowed heavily from classical Greece. Thus the hexagonal steeple is a double use of the

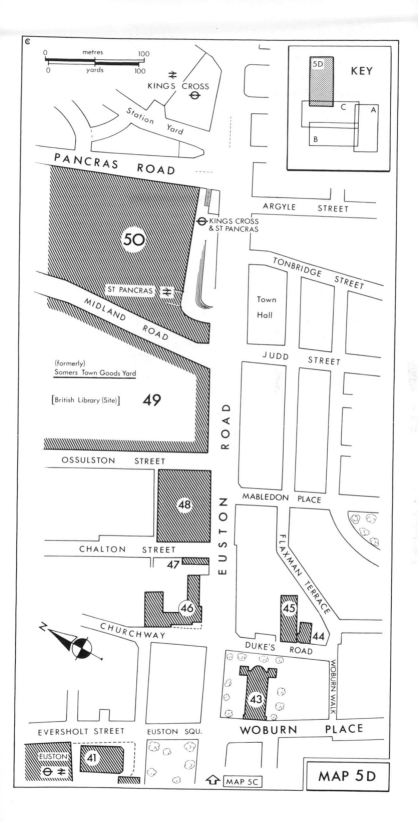

MAP 5D

*St Pancras Church
from Euston Road*
**(43)**

form of The Temple of the Winds, whilst the portico with its Ionic columns is taken from The Erectheum of the Acropolis, both structures sketched and measured on the ground in Greece by the younger Inwood in preparation for the design on the New Road.

The church itself is largely of brick, with an outer shell of Portland Stone, with most of the small decorative details fashioned in artificial stone of the Coade type. Aligned as it is parallel with the Euston Road, the buildings at the head of Woburn Place unfortunately block direct views of the church from the west, which could have been quite imposing. What is seen is still impressive, and the feature which must surely stick in peoples' minds must be the giant proportioned draped figures—caryatids—which appear to support the roof of the short wings at the east end. Again, these are borrowed from The Hall of the Caryatids in Athens. Like other details, the figures are fashioned in terracotta, and are hollow.

The broad steps to the entrance from Woburn Place, and the whole area behind the giant Ionic columns, are made up of large slabs of what appears to be Cornish Granite (there are large white feldspar crystals standing up like pebbles from the worn surfaces). Rough-dressed, the granite has flaked locally, possibly as a result of rising damp and localised corrosion effects produced by mineral salts in the groundwater. Turning to the Portland Stone columns, here we see the usual contrasts between the broad channelled bases which are very white, pitted by drips and corroded, and the vertical surfaces which tend to be darker in hue and surface-crazed (a condition already noted in the stonework of University College). The decorative mouldings, which include egg-and-dart patterns, acanthus leaves and rosettes, all look too crisp and brittle in contrast to the natural stone, thus proclaiming that they are indeed artificial stone paste. The judgement is not always an easy one to make, except in terms of these weathering characteristics seen about the doors. Inside, the church is surprisingly simple in comparison with some city churches which we have discussed so far. The internal space is undivided, but compressed by low galleries. The small side windows let in only suffused light, which all helps to focus attention upon the well-lit altar, about which we find a richness of

*Weathered Portland Stone base to column (43)*

antique marbles and gilding as the main decoration of the church.

The church survives in a local setting which is of the same period, which we can best appreciate if we walk down Woburn Place and then turn into Woburn Walk, a paved pedestrian sanctuary lined by uniformly scaled bow-window shops—brick with stucco facings, and very restrained. This provision of small shops was a commercial touch in the Cubitt plan of 1822–1830 to meet the needs of the new terraces to the south. Once again, in the paving to the Walk, we could dwell upon the sedimentary patterns such as fine scale ripple-marks and close spaced laminations within the large Coal Measure flagstones, details which emerge more and more with continued wear. Turning into Duke Street, we come upon yet more of the giant paving slabs, extending unbroken across the entire width of the elevated pavement on the west

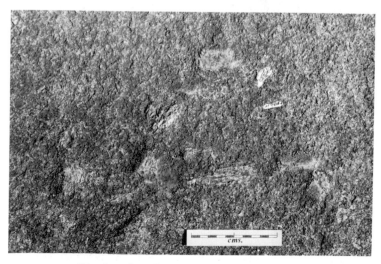

*Weathered granite step, St Pancras Church (43)*

The Place, Duke Street (**45**)

side of the street. Hereabouts, the high-standing kerbstones are a blend of blue basalt and the darker, slightly veined diorite which is probably from the Channel Isles, but on the opposite side, they change to being a wide range of different granites and gneisses.

On that same side, stand a group of late-Victorian buildings which almost inevitably involve terracotta. In **Grafton Mansions** built in 1890 (**44**), the material is just a small supplement to brick overall, but next door, in what used to be the Drill Hall of The Artists' Rifles (1888), now '**The Place**' (**45**), we see terracotta in its customary diversity of form—complex mouldings, crests, tablets bearing the date, and lettered signs, all in a fiery red colour. The building itself is of interest, in that it was designed by Sir Robert Edis, sometime colonel of The Artists' Rifles, but also responsible for other terracotta buildings which we have seen in other walks, such as No. 10 Fleet Street, and Nos. 100–101 Piccadilly.

Back in Euston Road, the **Elizabeth Garrett Anderson Hospital** (**46**) in its older part (1866), is of yellow stock brick, with quoins and window surrounds of contrasting red brick. One of the many problems of

this famous hospital has been the poor quality of the stone dressings including the window sills, but now that this detail has been restored and the brickwork cleaned of years of accumulated grime, the building positively glows in the company of some rather stoneless and dull neighbours. As it is, locally it is the kerbstones which sustain geological interest, many of them being blue Channel Islands diorite (as in Duke Street) or otherwise the dull red Mountsorrel Granite from Leicestershire, with just the occasional grey Cornish Granite with large and obvious large white orthoclase phenocrysts. Another red granite figures nearby in **The Rising Sun** (1899), the pub at the corner with Charlton Street (**47**). This is a typical late-Victorian public house with generous facing pillars of a Swedish red granite, either Imperial or Balmoral Granite, with large feldspar crystals and a deep red colour which goes well with the interior of dark polished wood and cut-glass mirrors. Facing The Rising Sun across the street, **St Pancras Library** (**48**), with its purpose of feeding the mind, is a more clinically simple building of the 1960's—a tall tower clad in smooth Portland Stone, some of it quite

St Pancras Library,
Euston Road (**48**)

shelly as the dark-weathering lines across the slabs demonstrates. The commercial part of the building, No. 110 Euston Road, has at its entrance steps and inclined slabs of Lake District Green slate as a sort of apron at pavement level. The locality for this stone is unknown, but it is clearly from the outcrop of the Borrowdale Volcanic Series of the central Lake District. Last seen in the Institute of Archaeology, here the slates show rusty-brown, included fragments which must be weathered volcanic ash which effectively pick out for us the actual bedding directions within the rock as opposed to the cleavage fracture surface. Perhaps it could be said that details here are best seen on wet days, when water streams over the surfaces.

We have now reached what used to be the site of **Somers Town Goods Yard** of the old Midland Railway (**49**), bomb damaged during the Second World War, cleared in post-war years and used for many years as a parking lot. In due course (1984), it is to become the site of the new British Library, but for the moment it allows generous views of the fully three-dimensional aspects of **St Pancras Station** (**50**), a build-

ing which could easily occupy us in several hours of study of its stonework. In terms of plans for its redevelopment or modification, the station is second only to Piccadilly Circus for controversy and divergent opinions. Most of the discussions focus upon the fronting hotel, leaving the simple and functional train-shed behind that front very much as it is, whether it be as a continuing rail terminus, or some kind of co-vered exhibition or sports arena. Be this as it may, having lost the battle of the Euston Arch, there exists a fairly broad-based insistence that the station *in toto*, right down to its richly finished booking hall wood-work should survive, come what may.

It is a well known fact that the great train shed was designed by the engineer Barlow to provide a simply supported roof arch over a site with a sub-surface goods depot beneath which there lay the Underground restricting the use of deep piling. To this end, he used the laterally placed girders made by the Butterley Iron-works in Derbyshire to support the high-arched single span roof of 243 ft. The geological fact to be wrung from all this is that the Butterley Company was one of the major

*St Pancras Station from Euston Road*

producers of ironwork of the Industrial Revolution in this country, and, like the more famous Coalbrookdale Company in Shropshire, was sited in the Derwent Valley of Derbyshire at a point where coal seams and blackband iron ores within the Coal Measure succession occurred in close proximity to one another.

Turning now to the famous hotel, the work of the architect George Gilbert Scott in designing and superintending the construction of the building towering above the Euston Road is well documented (in particular, Simmonds, 1975). What is less often discussed is the wide range of natural building stones which became an integral part of the architecture of this 'cathedral to the High Gothic', a point which is our principal interest. Jack Simmonds in his account judges that Scott's work was a powerful piece of showmanship which was just what the new and assertive Midland Railway needed to establish its position, coming as it did the second-last main line company to reach the capital. The argument could be extended to involve the stone it seems, in the fact that, with only one or two exceptions, all the quite striking natural stones employed by Scott

were to be found in the territory served by the new railway. In this way, the hotel became a kind of trade display for Mansfield New Red Sandstone, Peterhead Granite and Ketton and Lincolnshire Limestone, all of which arrived in London through the Somers Town Goods Yard nearby after 1865.

If we look at the fabric of the station, the principal contribution in sheer bulk, must be Nottinghamshire Red Brick, specially fired for the contract by Mr Grippe at Mapperly, just outside Nottingham. The bricks were made from Keuper Marl clays to Grippe's own patent process which involved their firing in an early version of a Hoffman continuously-fired kiln, using the waste gases to pre-heat chambers being brought into production from the cold state. Up to sixty million bricks, smooth-surfaced and dense, were required to sustain the building of the hotel, and they appear to have been supplied with relatively few delays due to bad weather (a seasonal problem in clay-pits), the smooth flow representing a major exercise of organisation over five years. The bricks seem to have retained their hard surface over the years and have emerged well from the part-cleaning of the

*Sandstone and limestone details of the Old Hotel Entrance St Pancras Station*

station of recent years (1981). Locally, however, in damper and darker corners, as will happen with the best of materials, there has been unsightly blistering and flaking of surface, the result of frosting, dampness and some corrosion from the atmosphere.

Stone dressings to the red brick come in the form of four different sedimentary rocks, three limestones and one sandstone, namely Ancaster Stone and Ketton Stone from the Middle Jurassic of Rutland and Lincolnshire, Magnesian Limestone from Nottinghamshire and, finally, New Red Sandstone from Mansfield in Nottinghamshire, all quarrying areas served by branch lines of the Midland. These stones are probably best seen in the western range of buildings from Midland Road round into the main entrance from Euston Road, but especially in the once-grand port cochère to the hotel, which juts out to the very edge of the Euston Road and its traffic. Here, two of the stones, Ancaster and Mansfield Red give the colour contrasts and slightly moorish touches to the whole design, contrasting with the red brick and the dark reds of the polished granite columns. The usual basis for recognising Ancaster

Stone is its tendency to show a horizontal banding which is in part a contrast between shelly and non-shelly limestone. This is well-seen in the pavement level windows on the Midland Road, but in the port cochère, the slightly yellower stone seen in the carved coat of arms (of the cities served by the Midland Railway) tends to be more homogeneous and even-grained, indicating that it was drawn from the truly 'freestone' levels of the same quarries, or possibly those at Ketton. With certain exceptions, much of the carving survives quite well, but the same can not be said for the red sandstone. This figured more often in the carved capitals to the granite pillars and shafts, and in the frieze which extends laterally at the same level. The carved peacocks with fully spread tails of this frieze and the curved brackets of the capitals, have suffered considerable loss of surface, an effect which often follows when rock types of very contrasting porosity and heat absorption are thrown into contact with one another. Red sandstone also forms the upright square pillars alongside and behind the granite columns, and in their larger surface area we can pick out sedimentary structures such

129

*Detail in Sandstone and limestone, Old Hotel Entrance*

as current bedding and small-scale slumps. We can also judge the grain-size and roundness of the sand grains by lightly stroking the surface and rolling the detached grains in the palm of the hand. Their free-rolling movement quickly demonstrates the well-rounded character of the grains, backing up their supposed origin as partly wind-blown sand dunes of Permo-Triassic times. As usual, this sandstone has suffered worst where it has been exposed to water flow from broken and leaking drain-pipes, but another cause for failure has been the use of the rock for slender shafts alongside the more massive granite columns. In this situation, the sandstone has been turned from lengths of stone quarried parallel with the bedding so that potential planes of parting run down the length of the shaft. As we see them in the east end archway (the exit from the main platform area of the station), several of these face-bedded shafts have split and in some cases have been clumsily repaired with a fiery red stone paste.

Magnesian Limestone is to be seen in the balustrade to the walls facing on to the Euston Road and in the very much reduced gateposts at the west-end entrance, where the stone was married with New Red Sandstone. Where it has not been cleaned in recent years the Magnesian Limestone has attracted thick crusts of black grime, but beneath can be seen the distinctive powdery

yellow crusting and, in some cases, an oolitic grain texture somewhat coarser than that seen in the Jurassic limestones mentioned earlier. As seen elsewhere in London, this is not a stone which stands up well to a polluted atmosphere and whilst all may now be changed with the Clean Air Act the damage has already been done to a considerable extent. As with the New Red Sandstone from Mansfield, the effect is generally one of a loss of sharp edges and crisp details, as well as a general eating back of the entire surface of blocks.

Yet another sedimentary rock makes its appearance in the long lengths of the steps which line the curving inclines from Euston Road to the main east end entrance. These are slabs of Coal Measure flagstones from West Yorkshire which, with the foot tread of many years, have begun to show up an internal sedimentary structure pattern which is sometimes small scale ripple-mark, sometimes ripple-drift, both emerging on the worn surfaces as concentric traces resembling grain in wood.

Turning now to the igneous rocks, the hotel and station contain a substantial amount of granite of one type of another, and indeed would have contained more had not Scott been curbed in his original intention by a minute of December 1866, in which he was asked 'to reduce the cost of decoration, especially in the use of granite columns' (Simmons,

1975). For this reason, granite was replaced by sandstone on the Pancras Road west front, and in the higher floor levels. The granite shafts and columns which were fixed are possibly thinner and less frequent than the overall design required. A similar economy probably ruled out the statues which should have occupied the niches liberally spread across the frontage. For all such economy, granite remains one of the splendours of St Pancras, particularly the substantial pillars of Shap Granite which stand at what was the main entrance to the hotel. In each of these we can clearly see the large orthoclase crystals, randomly orientated within the brown groundmass, which gives this granite its porphyritic texture. In several places too we can identify the dark coloured inclusions of Lake District Slate which form the 'heathen' of the quarrymen—the xenolith in the more classical jargon of the professional geologist. Whatever we call them, they eloquently testify to the fact that the granite entered the local crust as semi-molten material, capable of melting and digesting pre-existing rocks in its path. Set against the deeply weathered bases and capitals of New Red Sandstone, these polished granite columns offer visible proof of the lasting qualities of this one natural stone aginst the short-lived period of the other.

If we now move up the slope towards the giant arch which is the main access to the platforms and the booking hall, the hexagonal pillars which form the base to the arch are also of Shap Granite, but lack the high polished finish which the stone deserves. In a hammer-dressed finish, the familiar textures can just be made out through the greyness of the surfaces, which generally give a rather washed-out and jaded effect. Some of this impression may be due to recent cleaning operations (1980–81), which similarly transformed what is likely to be Peterhead Granite, seen in the shafts splitting the windows which open on to the passage-way. The rock has a paler-than-usual background (the normally pink orthoclase feldspars being grey), against which the patches of quartz stand out as almost black in tone. Other pillars show the normal even-toned pink colour of Peterhead Granite, this rock alternating with the porphyritic Shap Granite in the columns. At higher levels in the hotel, when you reach the uppermost floors, some of the windows are split by shafts of a darker blue-grey granite which is Cairngall Granite, a variant of the more familiar pink Peterhead Granite, linked with it through the common presence of the same stumpy pink orthoclase crystals, Proving this point in St Pancras must be a matter for trust, or the scanning of the upper floors with good binoculars.

More granites come into the paving and the kerbstones of the station, to add to the range of rock types available. In the paving to the port cochère, for example, broad cross slabs, worn smooth by carriage wheels, are of a Cornish Granite, recognisable on account of its very large white orthoclase phenocrysts. By way of contrast, just along-

*Pale, cleaned surface of Shap Granite, St Pancras Station*

side are dull blue setts of basalt which effectively set off the paler Cornish rock. Moving up the station approach, there are quite a number of different rocks in the kerbing, including the dull red Mountsorrel Granite from Charnwood Forest. Not far away, there are smoother grey-green slabs which appear to be pieces of Swithland Slate from the Precambrian succession of the same area. Swithland Slate is a true slate, the product of deformation and stress which altered what was originally a muddy sediment to the extent that the platy mineral components became aligned to the prevailing stresses, producing the cleavage within the rock. This same cleaved rock type provided some of the original slating for the hotel, remaining visible mainly in the attic storey roofs where they can be identified by their grey-green colour as well as their slightly lumpy appearance. In contrast, if you look to the western end of the building, you will see that there, the roof has been renewed in very smooth silver-grey slates from Dinorwic in North Wales.

Clearly in its total fabric, St Pancras offers us the widest range of rock types of any Victorian building in London from just a cursory survey of the accessible parts of the exterior. The possibility that there could be more to discover was brought home in the course of the recent cleaning operation, (1980–81). Looking at the upper floors in the company of Mr Cyril Mawer, a man seemingly dedicated to stone and stonework for both work and pleasure, it seemed that several distinct Jurassic limestones might be identified coming from the eastern counties. As it is, with the renewal work of those months suspended for lack of funds, the station now stands as a monument in another sense, demonstrating clearly to the passing public a 'before' and 'after' contrast, and to the geologists the profound effects of weathering in different rock types.

St Pancras Station with all its character and impact would be difficult to follow, and for this simple reason, it is an appropriate point at which to end our walk, and indeed this series of walks in the City.

*The trees of a Bloomsbury Square (Gordon Square) and the Euston Road skyline from the roof of University College, London.*

# REFERENCES

Including titles referred to in the text and others which back up the general themes of the walks accounts.

ARKELL, A. J. 1948. *Oxford Stone,* Faber.

ASHURST, J. & F. G. DIMES, 1977. *Stone in Building: its use and potential,* Architectural Press.

ATTERBURY, P. & L. IRVINE, 1979. *The Doulton Story,* Doulton, Stoke.

BAILEY, N. 1981. *Fitzrovia,* Historical Pub. Camden Hist. Soc.

BARKER, F. & R. HYDE, 1982. *London as it might have been,* John Murray.

BARNARD, J. 1973. *The decorative Tradition,* Architectural Press.

BONIFACE, M. 1981. *Hotels & Restaurants, 1830 to present day* H.M.S.O. Roy. Comm. Hist. Monuments.

BURTON, M. 1980. *Recut Jasper is fit for a new life,* Stone Industries.

BURTON, M. 1982. *Angel Court,* Stone Industries.

BYRON, A. 1981. *London Statues,* Constable.

CROSBY, T. 1970. *The necessary Monument,* Studio Vista.

DANGERFIELD, J. & J. R. Hawkes, 1981. *The Variscan Granites of S.W. England: additional information,* Proc. Ussher Soc.

ELSDEN, J. V. & J. A. Howe, 1923. *The Stones of London,* Colliery Guardian.

FLETCHER, G. 1981. *London at my feet.* Daily Telegraph.

GROESSENS, E. 1981. *L'Indutrie du Marbre en Belgique,* Mem. Inst geol. Univ. Louvain.

HAWKES, J. R. & J. DANGERFIELD, 1978. *The Variscan Granites of S.W. England: a progress report,* Proc. Ussher Soc.

HOBHOUSE, H. 1971. *Thomas Cubitt; master builder,* Macmillan.

JACKSON, A. J. 1969. *London's Termini,* David & Charles.

JONES. E. & C. WOODWARD, 1983. *A Guide to the Architecture of London,* Weidenfeld & Nicholson.

JONES. L. 1979. *Angel Court cladding,* Ove Arup. Journ.

McKEAN, C. & T. JESTICHO, 1976 *Guide to Modern Buildings in London, 1965–75,* Academy Editions.

MALTBY, S. et al. 1983. *Alfred Waterhouse, 1830–1905,* R.I.B.A.

NAIRN, I. 1964. *Modern Buildings in London,* London Transport.

PEVSNER, N. 1962. *The Buildings of England—London I, the Cities of London & Westminster,* Penguin.

REDFERN, R. A. 1979. *Exploring Mull's unusual Coastline,* Country Life.

SERVICE, A. 1979. *The Architects of London, their buildings from 1066 to present day,* Architectural Press.

SIMMONS, J. 1968. *St Pancras Station,* George Allen & Unwin.

SMITHSON, A. & P. SMITHSON, 1968. *The Euston Arch, and the growth of the London, Midland & Scottish Rly,* Thames & Hudson.

SUMMERSON, J. 1976. *The Victorian Rebuilding of the City of London,* London Journal.

# GLOSSARY

Including some stone names listed in the Index

ACID ROCKS: igneous rocks relatively rich in silica to the extent of having free quartz as a component mineral. Granite is an acid rock.

ASHLAR: a term descriptive of masonry meaning a smooth surface finish. Even-grained, well cemented stones, either sandstones or limestones, allow such a finish.

AXE-DRESSED (or HAMMER-DRESSED): a term for masonry which has been pecked or scored to give a rough surface finish. Granites and igneous rocks are often so treated.

BASALT: a dark coloured basic lava, the fine grained equivalent of gabbro or dolerite in the sense of chemical composition. Often used for kerbstones or paving setts, identified as the distinctly black or blue stones.

BASIC ROCKS: igneous rocks relatively poor in silica and so normally lacking free quartz as a component mineral. Gabbro and basalt are typical basic igneous rocks.

BATH STONE: a Middle Jurassic limestone (usually an oolite) of orange-brown colour. The traditional building stone of Bath and Cotswold towns.

BEDDING: a natural layering in rocks of sedimentary origin, reflecting short breaks in deposition. The natural planes of parting in most rocks.

BIOCLASTIC: a descriptive term implying that a rock, usually a limestone, is made up of calcareous shell debris.

BRECCIA: a rock consisting of angular broken fragments as distinct from the rounded fragments found in conglomerates. May be the result of rock rupture or short distance transport of rock debris.

CARBONIFEROUS: a period of geological time (a system). About 360–285 million years ago.

CALEDONIAN: a mountain building period recognised by geologists as occurring about the end of the Lower Palaeozoic between 450 and 350 million years ago. Responsible for the Grampian Highlands of Scotland, and the mountains of the Lake District and North Wales.

CLADDING: and architectural term for non-load-bearing slabs of rock attached to the structural frame of a building.

CLEAVAGE: a platy structure in fine grained metamorphic rocks, induced by stresses during deformation. Often confused with natural bedding.

COADE STONE: the best known of artificial stones, being a fired clay, probably containing crushed feldspar, but the precise formula unknown. Much used in 18th and 19th centuries.

COAL MEASURES: a late Carboniferous time period during which the coal bearing rocks of Britain and Europe were formed.

CORNICE: an architectural term for a moulded projection which can cap a wall, usually at roof or floor levels.

CRETACEOUS: a period of geological time, best known for the familiar rock type, chalk. This pure limestone was developed widely across Europe about 65–70 million years ago.

DEVONIAN: a period of geological time, recognised originally for the rocks of Devon. About 360 to 400 million years ago.

DIORITE: a coarse grained igneous rock composed of plagioclase feldspar, hornblende and biotite mica. Usually quartz-free and dark in colour.

DOLERITE: a medium grained igneous rock, basic in composition. Dolerite has much the same composition as basalt, and has been widely used for tarmacadam surfaces, kerbstones and cobbles (dark blue in colour).

DOULTON WARE: a popular ceramic tile with a strong glazed surface. The same material was moulded into decorative details for buildings in the late 19th, early 20th centuries.

EXFOLIATION (or SPALLING): a weathering habit in stone whereby crusts or splinters flake from surfaces like the skins of an onion.

FELDSPAR: an important group of rock-forming minerals present in all igneous rocks and some metamorpnic and sedimentary rocks. Alumino-silicates of potassium, sodium or calcium, typical members are orthoclase (K-rich), albite Na-rich) and anorthite (Ca-rich).

GABBRO: a coarse-grained basic igneous rock, similar in grain size to some granites, but not so poryphritic. Lacking free quartz, but rich in pyroxene and olivine. Gabbros are invariably dark in colour. Altered gabbros are the rocks most often referred to as 'Black Granite'

GLAUCONITE: a pale to dark green potash-rich clay mineral, commonly found as distinct grains in sedimentary rocks. Formed only in marine conditions, it is the colouring agent in 'greensands'.

GNEISS: a strongly banded and coarse-grained metamorphic rock, recognised by its alternate layers of dark and light coloured minerals.

GRANITE: a coarse-grained acid igneous rock, light coloured on account of the proportion of free quartz present in its make-up. Principal minerals are quartz, orthoclase feldspar, hornblende, muscovite and biotite micas. Often porphyritic.

GREENSAND: both the name of a rock type (a sandstone containing the green mineral glauconite) and of stratigraphical units within the Cretaceous rocks of southern England.

HAM HILL STONE: a coarse-grained bioclastic limestone of Jurassic age, quarried for grand buildings in the south west of England since late Middle Ages. A rich corn-coloured stone.

IGNEOUS ROCK: rocks formed by the cooling of a hot melt within the crust (from the latin *ignis*, fire).

JASPER: an extremely hard rock, consisting almost entirely of fine grained silica, possibly associated with lava eruptions.

JURASSIC: a period of geological time during which the rocks familiar to us in the Cotswolds and Dorset Coast were formed. The source of many excellent limestone building stones with local names (Guiting Stone, Ketton Stone, Ancaster Stone, etc.)

KENTISH RAG (-STONE): a tough glauconitic calcareous sandstone, quarried from the North Downs of Kent and Surrey since Roman times. The original building stone of the City of London.

LAKE DISTRICT GREEN SLATE: a fine grained green volcanic ash, metamorphosed and cleaved to slate form. Used as cladding to buildings, either in rough riven surfaces or rubbed smooth.

LARVIKITE: a distinctive variant of syenite; a coarse-grained igneous rock with distinctive iridescent feldspar crystals usually giving a shimmering blue cast to the rock. Comes only from Larvik district on Oslo Fjord.

MARBLE: to the stone trade, any rock which will take and retain a surface polish, consequently, igneous rocks and sedimentary rocks can be 'marble'. To a geologist, the term is restricted to limestones which have undergone metamorphism by heat and/or pressure so that the calcite has been recrystallised.

MAGNESIAN LIMESTONE: a buff coloured limestone, containing a proportion of magnesium within its make-up (a double carbonate rock). The best known sources are quarries in Nottinghamshire and South Yorkshire.

METAMORPHISM: geological processes which produce a changed form for either igneous or sedimentary rocks. Forces involved include heat and pressure. Gneiss and marble are metamorphic rocks.

MICA: a rock-forming mineral with a flat, platy habit. There are two main varieties, muscovite mica is silvery and transparent, biotite mica is dark brown or black.

OLIVINE: a rock-forming mineral group, silicates of iron (Fe) and magnesium (Mg), hence the term ferromagnesian for this type of mineral (along with pyroxenes). Olivine is present in most basic igneous rocks such as dolerite or basalt.

OOLITE: a form of limestone with a distinctive 'cods roe' texture resulting from lime grains becoming coated with a skin of lime creating an even-sized pellet. Oolites are freestones.

ORTHOCLASE: a rock-forming mineral of the feldspar family, being the potash (K) feldspar. Commonly found in acid igneous rocks, including granites.

ORDOVICIAN: a period of geological time, named after the native tribes of North Wales where rocks of this age are best developed. About 500 to 438 million years ago.

PALAEOZOIC: a geological era spanning the time period 600 to 240 million years, and including the first strong evidence of ancient life.

PILASTER: an architectural term for a vertical, projecting column or pillar attached to a wall surface.

PORPHYRY: a textural term for a rock containing large crystals set within a groundmass of finer grained character. The Porphyry of classical antiquity combined this texture with a rich purple colour.

PORTLAND STONE: a dense creamy-white limestone of Upper Jurassic age widely used in public buildings in Britain. Possibly the best known building stone in Britain, all derived from Portland Island, south of Weymouth on the Dorset Coast.

PRECAMBRIAN: a vast extent of geological time preceding a period, the Cambrian, which contains the earliest commonly occurring fossils.

QUARTZITE: a tough, durable stone, entirely composed of the mineral quartz, and in which the grains are welded together more effectively than in most sandstones. Some quartzites are metamorphosed sandstone.

QUOIN: an architectural term for dressed stones strengthening the angles of a building. Sometimes there is an alternation of large and small blocks.

RAGSTONE: a rough-textured limestone, the roughness often being created by included shell fragments. A stone not usually suitable for fine ashlar finishes.

ROACH: a cavity-rich variant of Portland Stone, the cavities resulting from the solution of shells to leave vacant casts.

RUSTICATION (ROCK-FACED): a masonry term for a rough external finish intended to simulate a natural rock surface.

SCHIST: a metamorphic rock with a strongly foliated ('leaved') character, rich in the mineral mica which is in part responsible for the foliation. Originally a shale or mudstone, altered by heat and pressure.

SERPENTINITE: a much-altered ultrabasic or basic igneous rock in which metamorphism has altered the ferromagnesian minerals to the fibrous end product serpentine and/or chlorite. Usually dark green or almost black, the rock is usually criss-crossed by white veins of calcite, giving the serpent-skin pattern and lustre from whence the name.

SYENITE: a coarse grained igneous rock, rich in alkalis but poor in silica, hence usually lacking free quartz. Larvikite is an example.

STRING COURSE: an architectural term for a thin projecting strip running across the face of a building.

TRACE FOSSILS: tracks and trails in sedimentary rocks created by burrowing organisms whilst the sediment was still soft.

TRAVERTINE: a calcareous spring deposit, full of cavities and voids, built up much in the same manner as stalagmite deposits in caves. Most travertines are of relatively young geological time periods, Tertiary or Recent, and most commercial travertines come from Mediterranean countries, particularly Italy.

TRIASSIC: a period of geological time, named in Europe for its invariable well-defined division into three parts of different character. About 248 to 213 million years ago.

ULTRABASIC: a category of igneous rocks poorer in silica than Basic igneous rocks (q.v.).

# INDEX OF STONE NAMES

It will always be the aim of the Geologist to identify rock types, and to be able to say something about the place of origin of a particular stone. The task is not always easy or straightforward. Our experience is of necessity limited to but a few rocks from field study, and most of these will be British. Records of stone used in the accounts of architects tends to be pretty basic or a simplified version of information from the Stone Trade. Their language is colourful, descriptive, and sometimes deliberately evasive. From all such sources, names have been attached to certain well known buildings, and are offered here as examples for comparison as you conduct your own investigations.

*Stones referred to in Book One are in italic.*

# INDEX OF PRINCIPAL BUILDINGS